THE COMPLETE GUIDE TO
CARD
MAKING

THE COMPLETE GUIDE TO
CARD
MAKING

100 techniques with 25 original projects and a template gallery

S A R A H   B E A M A N

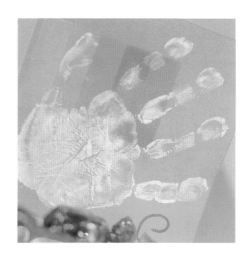

COLLINS & BROWN

FOR RUSSIE WORBOYS, 1912–2001.

an inspiration...

First published in Great Britain in 2003
by Collins & Brown Limited
64 Brewery Road
London N7 9NT

A member of **Chrysalis** Books plc

9 8 7 6 5 4 3 2

British Library Cataloguing-in-Publication Data:
A catalogue record for this book
is available from the British Library.

ISBN 1 85585 979 3

Conceived, edited and designed by Collins & Brown Limited

Editor: Kate Haxell
Designer: Roger Daniels
Photography: Matthew Dickens
Illustrations: Kuo Kang Chen and Dominic Harris

Reproduction by Classicscan Pte Ltd
Printed and bound in Malaysia by Times Offset Ltd

Distributed in the United States and Canada by
Sterling Publishing Co.
387 Park Avenue South, New York, NY 10016, USA

Contents

Introduction

I have been making cards for many years, for personal use and professionally, and I still find it an exciting and absorbing occupation. The best thing about making your own cards is the freedom it offers to express creative thoughts and ideas in your own unique way.

A hand-made card is a true sign of your affection for someone. Whether it is a simple stamped design on a thank-you note or an embroidered and be-jewelled birthday greeting, the fact that you have taken the time to make it yourself will mean something to the recipient.

You may not think that you are 'artistic', but to make a card – a really lovely card – you don't have to be. The thing to remember is that there really are no set rules, no specific rights and wrongs, in cardmaking. You don't need to have years of experience and expertise, though you will find that a little confidence goes a long way. Maybe the most important asset for any cardmaker is an eye for detail. A well-made card with careful and considered decoration is the key to a successful result.

It may be that every Christmas you have vowed to make your own cards; for every loved-one's birthday you have planned to create something special, but in the end inspiration has failed you and you have gone out and bought a less-than-satisfactory card. Well in this book you have at your fingertips 100 tried-and-tested techniques, along with dozens of additional inspirational ideas for making your own cards. You will find quick and easy ideas for when you are in a hurry and more elaborate techniques and projects for when time is on your side. There really are no more excuses.

If you have never made a card before, then begin at the beginning. The first two chapters are full of practical techniques to get you started and prepare you for the dozens of decorative techniques that follow.

Towards the back of the book you will find 25 original projects that you can follow; the templates you will need are in the Templates section. I hope that these projects will inspire you to create your own original cards.

If you have been making cards for years, then I hope that you will find here many techniques and design ideas that are new to you. Whether you prefer making simple, modern cards, or revel in constructing elaborate designs, there are techniques to suit your taste.

Whether you are a novice or an enthusiastic card maker, remember to keep your eyes open for ideas and inspiration, they can strike at any time! Notice things – it may be a particular combination of colours that catches your attention, or an arrangement of objects that pleases you. Even a sense of shape and proportion you find interesting might inspire a card. Think about what appeals to you and why it does so.

Store these ideas away somewhere for future use. Make notes if you feel so inclined, they will be useful one day when you are faced with a blank piece of card and have an equally blank mind. As you become more practised and begin to 'get your design eye in', you will arrive at a set of formulae for proportion, shape and style that works for you and almost always leads to a pleasing result.

Above all, enjoy yourself. Card making should be fun and satisfying and it should give you as much pleasure as it does the recipient of your endeavours. It might be that you are only making a card, but let it be the most beautiful card possible.

Sarah Beaman

Tools and materials

You do not need a lot of equipment to start making cards. The basics are a pencil, soft eraser (a mouldable putty rubber is ideal), steel rule, set square, craft knife (a retractable blade is safest – slide it in when you are not using it), cutting mat, table knife, and whatever you want to decorate the card with.

All the equipment you need is available from art and craft shops (see Suppliers, page 159), so buy items as you need them. Before you start a project, make sure that you have everything that you need, there is nothing more irritating than having to stop because you are missing a piece of equipment.

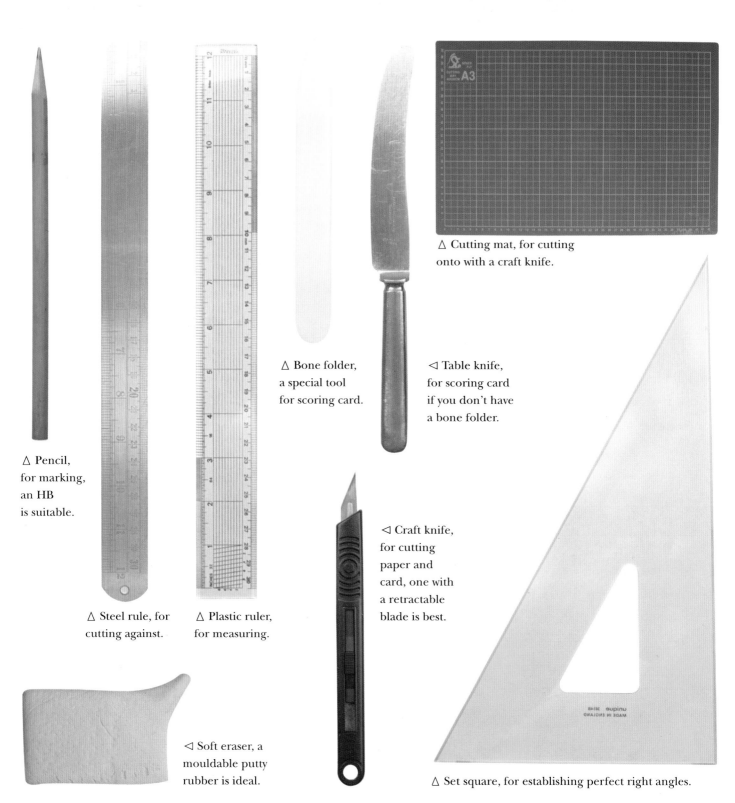

△ Cutting mat, for cutting onto with a craft knife.

△ Bone folder, a special tool for scoring card.

◁ Table knife, for scoring card if you don't have a bone folder.

△ Pencil, for marking, an HB is suitable.

△ Steel rule, for cutting against.

△ Plastic ruler, for measuring.

◁ Craft knife, for cutting paper and card, one with a retractable blade is best.

◁ Soft eraser, a mouldable putty rubber is ideal.

△ Set square, for establishing perfect right angles.

◁ Large scissors, for cutting many different materials.

◁ Small scissors, for cutting detail.

◁ Pinking shears, for cutting zigzag edges on many different materials.

◁ Decorative-edge scissors, for cutting shaped edges on a variety of materials other than fabric.

△ Blunt-toothed tracing wheel, for piercing paper and card.

△ Needle-toothed tracing wheel, for piercing paper and card.

△ Paintbrushes, for applying colour and water.

△ Brush pen, for colouring edges and embellishing stamps and stencils.

△ Watercolour pencils, for colouring edges.

◁ Ink, for decorating paper.

△ Paper adhesive, for sticking paper, the glue- stick type is best.

△ All-purpose adhesive, for sticking many different materials, the gel-type is best.

△ Glue pen, for sticking tiny items.

△ Spray adhesive, for sticking delicate items and lightweight paper.

△ Fabric adhesive, for sticking fabric, the water-based type is best.

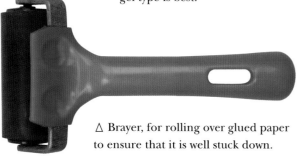

△ Brayer, for rolling over glued paper to ensure that it is well stuck down.

◁ Embossing tool, for embossing paper into a stencil.

◁ Embossing pen, for embossing with powder.

◁ Gilding pen, for gilding fine detail or freehand designs.

△ Double-sided tape (top) and masking tape (below), for sticking many different materials.

△ Vari-coloured twisted hand-embroidery thread, for stitching on card and fabric and making cord.

△ Vari-coloured stranded hand-embroidery thread, for stitching on card and fabric and making cord.

△ Tapestry yarn, for stitching on card and fabric and making cord.

△ Vari-coloured machine embroidery thread, for stitching on card and fabric.

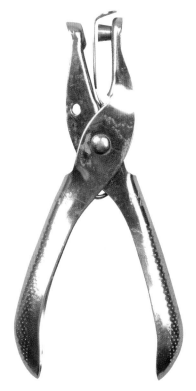

△ Leather punch, for punching different-sized holes in many materials.

△ Single-hole punch, for punching holes in paper and card.

△ Slot punch, for punching slots in paper and card.

△ Needle vice, for holding a needle while piercing paper, card or metal foil.

Techniques

In this section you will find 100 practical and creative techniques for making and decorating cards. The techniques are divided into chapters, each containing several ideas for using particular tools or materials. From decorating paper to sophisticated embossing techniques, here is everything you need to know to create your own cards.

The first chapters deal with the more practical aspects of making a card. Learn to make a card blank and an envelope to complement and to fit the card. Once you have made a card blank you need to decide how to treat the edges, if at all, before decorating the front of the card, and there are nine different edging techniques to choose from. Once this decision has been made you can move on to the front of the card.

A practical chapter on choosing the right adhesives for different materials is followed by a dozen more chapters exploring different decorative techniques. Each technique is explained in detail and tip boxes give both practical advice and inspirational ideas for using a particular technique in a different way.

You can work through the chapters in order or dip in and out of them at will, depending on what you want to do. The final chapter includes relief presentation ideas for displaying your work to best advantage.

Making card blanks

A blank card is the essential element for every technique and project in this book. You can buy pre-cut and scored card blanks from craft suppliers, these are useful if you want to produce a number of cards. However, they are available in a limited range of colours and sizes and may not be appropriate for the project you want to make. If you want a non-standard sized card, an unusual colour or particular type of paper, then you will need to make your own card blank. It's an easy task, but it's important to do it accurately and carefully, or the blank will look untidy, which is not a good starting point for any card.

1 Choosing card and paper

However simple the design of a card, choosing the right card or paper to start with can make the difference between a good and an exquisite job. There is a diverse selection of papers and cards available by the sheet or roll. Some basic knowledge of the qualities of paper and card will help you to choose the right material for a particular project.

Paper falls mainly into two categories; hand-made and machine-made. Hand-made paper has become increasingly popular and more widely available in recent years. There is a huge selection to choose from and more unusual papers have inclusions such as flower petals, grasses, wood, newsprint or metallic flecks, or long, visible fibres of silk or plant matter.

Although these special papers aren't mass-produced, many of them are not prohibitively expensive and they really can add another dimension to your card designs.

The process of making paper on a machine can give quite different results. Machine-made papers all have one particularly important characteristic: the individual fibres tend to align with each other and run in the same direction (in hand-made papers they settle in different directions). This is called the 'grain' and working with the grain of the paper will make life easier and give you better results.

To see this for yourself, take a piece of ordinary photocopy or computer paper. Crease the paper first lengthways, then widthways. If you look closely at the creases, one of them will look cleaner and sharper. The paper has creased most neatly in the direction of the grain. Try this out on a variety of papers as you come across them. As you develop a feel for it, it will not be necessary to crease the paper. Just fold it lightly first in one direction, and then in the other. If you apply gentle pressure it is possible to feel the different

▽ *A selection of hand-made papers including papers with inclusions (second, fourth and fifth from left), and papers with long fibres (first and eighth from left).*

resistances. The fold with the least resistance is running in the direction of the grain.

The grain can be particularly important if you tear the edges of a card. Tear a piece of everyday paper first lengthways and then widthways. You will see that you get a straighter tear running with the grain and a much more ragged tear across the grain.

Being aware of the characteristics and qualities of the materials you use will help to ensure that you get the best results from your efforts.

The abbreviation 'mic', short for 'microns', applies to the physical thickness of the paper, 1000 microns equals 1mm. Don't worry too much about thickness, be guided by weight instead.

Unless you are making a run of cards, paper size is probably not going to trouble you too much either. Paper is sold in range of standard sizes and for a single card the smaller sizes might not need further cutting, just scoring and folding. For larger cards you can buy sheets of paper that you can cut up to suit a project.

△ *A selection of machine-made papers including metallic paper (fifth from top), and heavily textured paper (eighth from top).*

2   Choosing card shapes

If you are going to use an existing envelope then this will dictate the finished size of the card. Non-standard sizes can look interesting and eye-catching and if you are going to make the whole thing from scratch, including the envelope, then virtually anything goes and you have the luxury of deciding. However, if you are going to post the card a sensible finished size is necessary.

So how do you decide what shape and size will work best for the card you want to make? Well, this is where making good aesthetic judgement comes in. It always helps to have a plan, so try to visualize the project in your head. You may already have an idea as to how you are going to decorate the card, or at least the materials and motifs you want to use.

There are two ways of working: you can decide on the card shape and then arrange materials within the defined space, or you can arrange the materials and then decide what shape card to mount them on. Sometimes, the items you are using will suggest the best format; for example, a long, thin pressed leaf will probably look best on a tall,

narrow card, while rounder motifs might look most effective on a square card.

Are you going to make an artwork that needs to be relief-mounted? Would it look better if it were framed by a border, or does it have rough edges that would be best concealed behind an aperture? Perhaps you are thinking of decorating the surface of the card itself?

Whatever your plan, designing an attractive card is all about balance and harmony. Analyze what you intend to use and ideally try out several options before you commit yourself. Remember that very often 'less is more'. It's not about filling all the available space, but arranging things sensitively within it.

△ *These are the three most common card shapes, though they can be found in almost any size.*

3 Measuring and cutting

Decide on the shape and size of the finished card. Work out the overall measurements, remembering that, for a comfortable fit, the folded card needs to be about 5mm (¼in) smaller all round than the envelope. It is important to be accurate when measuring, marking and cutting.

1 You must start out with a piece of paper with two straight edges at right angles to one another. If the paper doesn't have this, place a 90-degree set square in one corner and draw and then cut along both sides to establish a right angle. Using a pencil and ruler, measure and mark the height of the card. Measure up from a straight edge and make a pencil mark at the right height. Make light pencil marks so that they can easily be rubbed out afterwards with a soft eraser.

2 Position a set-square against the edge of the paper and at the marked height, draw a line the width of the unfolded card.

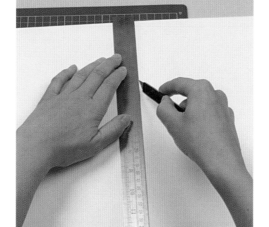
1

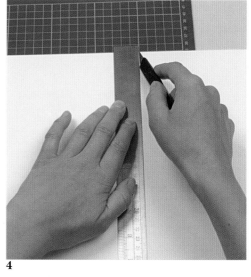
2

3

4

Getting it right

For the cleanest cut, use a steel rule and a craft knife with a new blade. A plastic or wooden ruler will quickly become damaged and edges cut along it will not be straight.

3 Turn the paper so that you will be cutting towards yourself. Place a steel rule along the pencil line and press it down firmly and evenly onto the paper, keeping your fingertips well out of the way. Cut carefully along the pencil line with a craft knife. This is best done on a self-healing cutting mat. If you don't have one of these, ensure that the work surface is adequately protected with a wad of newspaper and some cardboard.

4 If you are going to be making cards regularly then a self-healing cutting mat is a good investment. Apart from protecting the work surface, many mats are printed with centimetre (or inch) gridlines that make measuring quick and easy. Rather than measuring and marking with a pencil, align a straight edge of the paper with a gridline on the mat. Count across the gridlines to the required width and position a steel rule along the appropriate gridline. Cut the paper carefully with a craft knife.

4 Single-fold cards

Whether you are making your own blanks, or
purchasing them ready-made, a single-fold card is
the type you will need for many projects. It offers
an adaptable area to mount a decoration on.

1 Measure the full width of the card along the top edge and lightly mark the halfway point with a pencil. Repeat along the lower edge. Marks need to be accurate and parallel if the card is to fold squarely. You can check them with a set-square or the grid on a cutting mat. It is best not to pencil right along the fold line, as it may prove difficult to remove the pencil mark later on.

2 Position the ruler between the two marked points and applying firm, even pressure, 'draw' along the edge of the ruler with the point of a bone folder. Rub out the pencil marks with a soft eraser.

3 If you don't have a bone folder, the back of a table knife creates an effective score line. The process is the same as for step 2, though it is advisable to do a test first to establish the correct amount of pressure to apply with the knife.

4 Form the card by carefully folding the paper along the scored line, creasing it between your fingers and thumb.

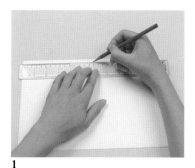
1

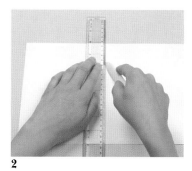
2

3

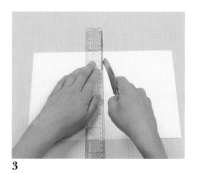
4

△ *Single-fold cards can be any shape and size. Tent-style*
cards, like the one on the left where the fold runs along the top
of the card, can present stability problems, as they tend to
collapse if the dimensions are not very carefully considered.

Getting it right

The score line is usually made on the outside of the card, but scoring the line on the inside can give a cleaner crease, particularly when using paper with loose or obvious fibres. If at all possible, do a few tests first on some scrap pieces of the paper you want to use, perhaps on a smaller scale. Bear in mind the effect that the grain of the paper (see *1 Choosing card and paper*, page 14) might have on the outcome. It is easier to fold the paper in the direction of the grain.

5 Three-panel cards

There are two types of three-panel card; a concertina card and an aperture card. An aperture card can be used to present needlecrafts, collage and other artworks on the centre panel, with one of the side panels forming the rear flap of the card and the other folding inward to cover the back of the middle panel. A concertina card can be decorated right across one side, as all three panels will be visible on the finished card.

An aperture card

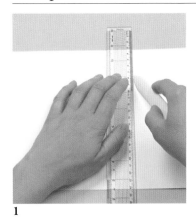

1

2

1 To make either card, carefully measure, mark and score the paper (see *3 Measuring and cutting*, page 16, and *4 Single-fold cards*, page 17). However, you must divide the paper into thirds rather than in half.

2 For an aperture card, score both lines on the same side of the paper. Trim 2mm (⅛in) off the outer edge of the right-hand panel, which will fold in to cover the back of the middle panel. The left-hand panel folds in to make the back of the card.

A concertina card

1

1 For a concertina card, make the first score line on one side of the paper and the second on the other side. Form the card by folding one panel forwards and the other one backwards.

6 Cutting square apertures

An aperture is a hole cut in a card in which you can display a piece of work. It can be cut in a three-panel card or a single-fold card, depending on the type of artwork you are framing. If you need to conceal the back of the artwork to cover raw or untidy edges, a three-panel card, or a separate panel taped inside a single-fold card, is the best solution.

In a three-panel card

1 Make an aperture card blank (see *5 Three-panel cards*, above). Lay the card out flat and, measuring with a ruler, lightly mark the centre point of the middle panel with a sharp pencil. Using a set square, lightly draw the aperture you want on the card. Make sure that it is central and upright. Double-check by measuring in from the edges of the card to the edges of the aperture on both sides.

1

2 Using a craft knife and a steel rule, carefully cut along the pencil lines to cut out the aperture. Always cut so that the aperture is to the right of the rule (or the left if you are left-handed) to protect the face of the card and ensure a clean edge. Move the card around between each cut so that you can clearly see the marks. Rub out the remaining pencil marks with a soft eraser. Mount the artwork (see *25 Masking tape*, page 33), and stick down the right-hand panel (see *26 Double-sided tape*, page 33).

2

Getting it right
You have greatest control when cutting towards you. Take great care not to cut beyond the corners of the aperture as this looks very untidy. If you find that a corner is still attached when you try to remove the aperture piece, do not pull it free. This will create fuzzy fibres that spoil the clean edge of the aperture. Use the point of the scalpel blade to cut cleanly through the last bit of paper.

▷ *You can mount almost any fairly thin artwork in an aperture, from a piece of embroidery to a simple coloured panel. Alternatively, the aperture can form part of a design in its own right. You could stitch across it, use it as a window to view an internal sheet or words through, or suspend decorations from its edges.*

▷ *Square aperture cards can be bought ready-made in a variety of sizes, including standard photograph sizes. These are particularly useful if you want to send the same picture – of a new baby, maybe – to a lot of people.*

In a single-fold card

1

2

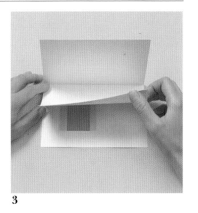

3

1 You can cut an aperture in a single-fold card and cover the back of the artwork framed in it with a separate panel of paper. This is useful if the paper is not large enough, or is too thick, to make a three-panel card. Make a single-fold card (See *4 Single-fold cards*, page 17), cut out the aperture out of the front panel and mount the artwork in it, as for a three-panel card. Cut another piece of paper the same size as the front panel and trim

2mm (⅛in) off the left-hand side, the side that will be next to the fold in the card. Stick a length of double-sided tape down each long side of the panel.

2 Lay the panel inside the card to check that it fits properly. Then peel the protective paper off the double-sided tape.

3 Lay the card face-down on the work surface with the fold away from you. This way you can

clearly see the three edges that the separate panel needs to align with. Provided you have only trimmed 2mm (⅛in) off the edge of the panel nearest the fold, you will find that having the card in this position means that the fold helps you align the panel correctly. Slip the separate panel, taped-side down, into the card and close the card down onto it. Press along the taped edges to ensure that they are firmly stuck down.

7   Cutting shaped apertures

Cutting shaped apertures such as hearts or stars is quite easy to do. Draw a shape or transfer a template to cut around (see 40 Transferring a template, page 43). Cutting circular or oval apertures is difficult, however, and they can look very amateurish. Practice and a steady hand are required. Whatever shape you want to cut, first make an aperture card blank (see 5 Three-panel cards, page 18).

1 Lay the card flat and using a pencil, lightly draw the aperture shape onto the middle panel of the card.

2 Place the card on a cutting mat and using a craft knife with a sharp, pointed blade, cut around the pencil line. Keep the blade as vertical as possible while you cut. Take your time and try to create a smooth shape. Rub out the remaining pencil marks with a soft eraser. Mount the artwork (see *25 Masking tape*, page 33), and stick down the right-hand panel (see *26 Double-sided tape*, page 33). You can also cut a shaped aperture in a single-fold card and use a separate panel to cover the back of the artwork (see *6 Cutting square apertures*, page 18).

1

2

△ *You can work out the size and shape of the aperture on a piece of tracing paper. When you are satisfied, transfer the image onto the card (see 40 Transferring a template, page 43).*

Getting it right

When cutting with either a blade or scissors, try to turn the item you are cutting while keeping the tool still. You are aiming to create a smooth and continuous line, with minimal stopping and starting. With scissors, use the whole length of the blades. With a craft knife, the point is very useful for tight corners and tricky details. If you do have to stop, ensure you start again in exactly the same place.

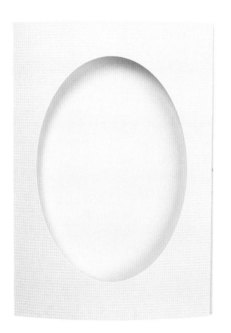

◁ *If you really do want a round or oval aperture with a smooth edge, it is best to buy a pre-cut blank, of which there are a wide variety available commercially. You can also buy cards with more decorative shaped apertures, including hearts and Christmas trees.*

8 Internal sheets

Many quality single-fold cards have an internal sheet on which the message can be written. Easy to achieve, this not only looks professional, but if you have used a heavily textured paper to make the card, then an internal sheet gives a smooth surface on which to write. Words can be printed onto the sheet before it is stuck in position, which is useful if you are making a batch of cards with the same message, such as invitations.

1 To make an internal sheet, follow the steps for making a single-fold card (see *4 Single-fold cards*, page 17). The internal sheet needs to be approximately 5mm (¼in) shorter and narrower than the card, so that when it sits inside the card there is a small border visible all around the edge. Cut the sheet to size with a craft knife and steel rule on a cutting mat.

2 Stick a strip of narrow double-sided tape (see *26 Double-sided tape*, page 33) along the folded front edge of the sheet, butting it right up against the fold.

3 Peel the protective paper off the double-sided tape.

4 Lay the open card face-down, with the front edge of the card towards you. Carefully position the internal sheet, taped-side down, matching the folds in the sheet and the card, and making sure that an even border of card is visible all around the edge. Press the sheet down to ensure that all of the tape makes contact with the card. Sticking the sheet to the front of the card, as opposed to the back, ensures that the sheet will open as the card is opened.

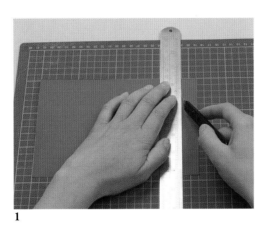

1

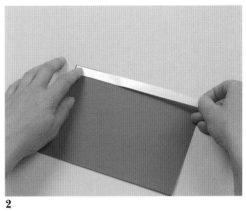

2

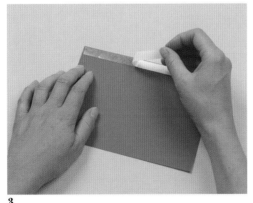

3

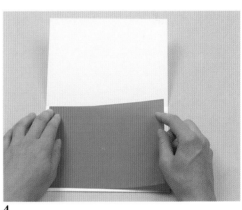

4

◁ *You can make the sheet in a complementary or contrasting colour to the main card. If you punch a row of holes or cut an aperture to reveal the sheet, it can become part of the decorative design of the card – pretty as well as practical.*

Getting it right

The internal sheet should be made from a lighter-weight paper – around 100gsm – suitable for writing on. Translucent papers work particularly well in this context and can look very effective. If necessary, make sure the quality is suitable for use with a printer or photocopier and print the sheets before you fold them.

Making envelopes

The envelope you present a card in is important; your efforts will not be set off to best advantage by a tatty envelope. If you can't find a suitable ready-made envelope, have a non-standard size card, or if you want to use a particular paper to co-ordinate with a card, then making your own envelope is the only option.

Also consider decorating the envelope to match the card; if you are stamping, for example, stamp a motif on the envelope, too.

If you want to post the card you must be able to write on the paper you make the envelope out of. It must also be strong enough to go through the mail and protect the card.

9   Envelopes from templates

A brown paper envelope may suit a rustic card, but it won't do a sophisticated modern card justice. However, it is easy to make an envelope to complement, and to fit, a card you have designed and made. Templates for the three most commonly used envelope shapes are on page 154. Use a photocopier to enlarge or reduce the one you choose as required.

1 Trace a template and transfer it onto the wrong side of the paper (see *40 Transferring a template*, page 43). Using scissors, cut out the envelope. If you are nervous about cutting straight lines, use a craft knife and steel rule on a cutting mat to cut the long straight edges and cut out the curves with scissors.

2 With the paper right-side down, lay a steel rule along one of the crease lines indicated on the template. Lift the flap up and fold it over the edge of the rule to make a neat crease. Repeat on all four sides to make four flaps, then open the flaps out flat again.

3 Fold in the two side flaps only and apply a thin line of paper adhesive (see *21 Paper adhesive*, page 31) – or special re-moistenable adhesive – along the edges that will be overlapped by the lower flap. Fold the lower flap up and press it

down onto the adhesive. Leave to dry.

4 The card can be sealed into the envelope in two ways. You can stick the top flap down with paper adhesive once the card is in the envelope, or you can use re-moistenable adhesive, as shown here. Paint a thin line of the adhesive along the inside edge of the top flap and leave it to dry. When you are ready to seal the card in the envelope, moisten the flap in the usual way to re-activate the adhesive, then stick the flap down.

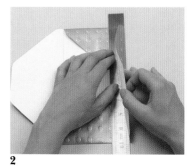

1

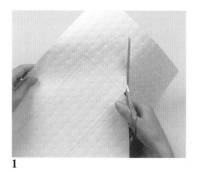

2

3

4

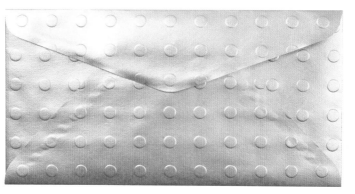

△ *An unusual paper that complements the card inside makes an interesting and imaginative envelope.*

Getting it right
When gluing the flaps, particularly the top flap, don't make the line of adhesive very thick or wide. It might spread too far and stick to the card inside, damaging it when it is removed.

10 Copying existing envelopes

Ready-made envelopes are available in an infinite range of sizes, qualities, colours and textures – but even if you find one the right size, it may not be the right colour. In this case, simply copy an envelope that is the right size in the paper of your choice.

1 Carefully take apart an envelope and flatten it out.

2 Lay it on the wrong side of the paper you want to make the new envelope from. Using a pencil and ruler, draw around the edges of the envelope as accurately as possible. Mark points to correspond to the crease lines, making sure that the marks will be visible once the envelope has been cut out.

3 Using a steel rule and a craft knife on a cutting mat, cut along the long straight edges. Cut around the curves freehand with the craft knife or scissors.

4 Align the steel rule with the marks indicating the crease on one of the flaps. Fold the flap over the edge of the rule to make a neat

crease. Repeat on all four sides to make four flaps, then open them out flat.

5 Fold the two side flaps in. Apply a thin line of paper adhesive (see *21 Paper adhesive*, page 31) along the edges of the bottom flap. Fold it up to overlap the side flaps and press it down. Leave to dry.

6 Once you have put the card inside, the top flap can be sealed with paper adhesive or re-moistenable adhesive (see *9 Envelopes from templates*, page 22), or a sticker, as used here. A sticker is not a very secure seal if you want to post the card, but it is fine if you are going to hand-deliver it. If you do want to post the card, glue the flap closed before applying the sticker.

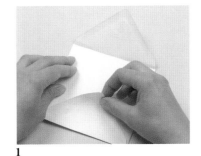
1

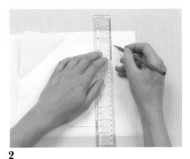
2

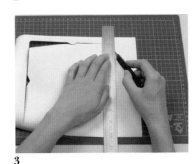
3

4

5

6

△ *You can make a flower sticker yourself by cutting a circle of clear, sticky-backed plastic and sticking a pressed flower to the centre of it, before sticking it onto the card.*

Ideas & inspiration

Co-ordinate the envelope with the card by continuing an element of the card decoration through onto the envelope. There is an enormous range of stickers on the market, so choose one to complement the card you have made.

Alternatively, try sealing the envelope with traditional sealing wax and a patterned seal (below far right).

11 Pillow envelopes

A card with three-dimensional elements will be spoiled if it is squashed in a flat envelope. Such cards are best hand-delivered in a pillow envelope, which is easy to make from thin card. Templates for pillow envelopes are on page 154. Enlarge or reduce the one you choose on a photocopier as required.

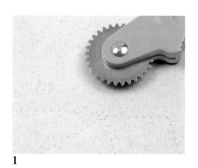

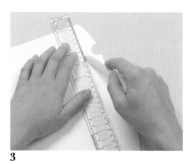
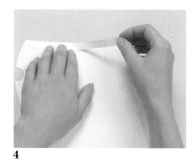
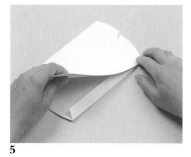

Ideas & inspiration

To add a finishing touch, tie the pillow envelope with ribbon. Keep it simple with linen tape and a tiny label (left), or use organza ribbon to tie a sumptuous bow (right). Alternatively, you can decorate the card before you make up the pillow envelope, see *Decorating paper* (pages 38–42) for some ideas.

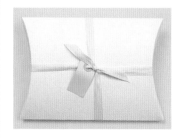

1 Trace the template and lay it on the right side of the card you want to make the envelope from. Run a dressmaker's tracing wheel over the template outline and crease lines to transfer them onto the card underneath. The indented lines will help you score the card and you do not have to make pencil marks that might be difficult to rub out. Use the wheel against a ruler along the straight edges and be careful not to make marks where they aren't needed, as you won't be able to remove them. Be especially careful around the indents, as the wheel can be tricky to manoeuvre around tight curves.

2 Remove the template and cut around the outer edges of the envelope with scissors, following the indented lines.

3 Using a bone folder and ruler, score the curved and straight lines indicated by the remaining indented lines. The scoring will cover the indentations made by the tracing wheel, so it is important to be accurate. Along the curved lines, move the ruler around a little bit at a time, so that it is always against the indentations and guiding the bone folder. To keep a scored line as smooth as

possible, don't lift the bone folder off a line until you reach the end of it.

4 Lay the envelope face down. Stick a strip of double-sided tape (see *26 Double-sided tape*, page 33) along the edge without the extended flap, trimming the tape at both ends where it meets the score lines so that it does not overlap them. The tape must not be wider than the extended flap or it will not be covered when the envelope is assembled. Peel the protective paper off the tape.

5 Fold the extended flap in. Fold the taped edge over it and press it down to ensure that the tape sticks to the card right along its length.

6 Use your fingers and thumbs to gently press on either side of the curved scored lines to help coax the end sections over. The sections with the indents must be folded over first, so that the envelope can be opened easily.

△ *This pillow envelope is made from card, but experiment with different materials, such as fine corrugated card or thin translucent plastics, to make envelopes that can be used to hold a small gift, as well as a card.*

Decorative edges

Although design ideas and decorative details will usually be concentrated on the front of a card, the edges also provide a good opportunity for additional enhancement or embellishment.

Some techniques, such as tearing and torn perforations, involve actually changing the nature of the edge. Other techniques, such as stitching and colouring, simply add decoration to the original edge. Whichever technique you choose, work it before you decorate the front of the card.

Many of the edging techniques can also be used on other areas of a card; around apertures or relief mounts, for example.

12 Using decorative scissors

Apart from dressmaker's pinking shears, the zigzag scissors most of us are familiar with, there are a huge variety of scissors with shaped blades that cut decorative edges. They are simple to use and provide quick and effective embellishments. Don't just use them on the outside of the card, consider using them around an internal sheet or the top flap of an envelope as well.

Cut the decorative edge close to the natural edge of the card. When you have closed the blades, open them out again and carefully re-align the pattern so that it runs consistently along the edge of the card.

Getting it right

You can also use these scissors to cut both sides of strips of paper for use in other techniques, such as collage (see *84 Creating a background*, page 84), or to make a border or frame.

△ *There are many different edges to choose from, but be cautious of using more than one on any card, or the effect will start to look untidy.*

13 Tearing against a rule

A distinctive deckle edge is usually found on hand-made papers and generally signifies a good-quality paper. The deckle can be used to make an attractive edge for a card or piece of mounted artwork. On many straight-edged papers a deckle-effect can be created using one of two techniques. If the paper is not too thick, you will probably be able to tear the edge against a rule.

Place a steel rule near to, and parallel with, the edge of the card. Make sure that the edge of the card protrudes approximately 10mm (½in) beyond the rule, so that you can hold it firmly between your forefinger and thumb. Press down very firmly on the rule with your left hand to stop it slipping. Tear the card by lifting the protruding edge and pulling it towards you a little at a time. If you are tearing a long length, move your left hand down the

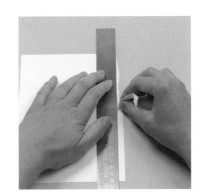

rule as you go, pressing hard to stop it slipping and to prevent the tear from running in the wrong direction across the card.

Getting it right

Paper with short fibres is easy to tear using this technique. However, practice is needed to get a good result on paper with inclusions or long, irregular fibres, such as mulberry paper. Pressure on the rule will help to prevent the tear from running in the wrong direction. When you approach a cluster of fibres you will feel some resistance, so stop tearing and pull sideways to draw the fibres out of the paper. Once the cluster has come free, you can tear as normal until you reach the next cluster.

△ *The grain direction, (see 1 Choosing card and paper, page 14), will have some bearing on both how the tear will look and how easy it is to do. It is more difficult to tear across the grain and you get a more ragged result than if you tear with the grain. If you want to tear in both directions, then some practice will be necessary. You also need to establish whether to tear on the back or front of the paper, as you get slightly different looks with each.*

14 Tearing using water

The second technique for creating a deckle-effect edge works particularly well on heavier-weight papers, or those that are not supple enough to tear. The edge looks slightly different to a torn edge, so try both and choose the one that you prefer.

1 Place a ruler parallel to the edge of the card. Make sure that the edge protrudes about 10mm (½in) beyond the ruler, so that you can hold it between your forefinger and thumb. Dip a fine paintbrush into water and paint a line along the ruler. Keep dipping the brush into the water to make sure that the line is evenly wet along its length. Allow the paper to absorb the water for a moment or two.

2 Hold the edge firmly, then gently pull it outwards to tear it away. The moistened fibres should separate quite easily. Leave to dry.

1

2

Getting it right
With thick paper you may need to paint more water over the line and leave it to soak in for up to a minute before it is wet enough to pull away.

▷ *Always create a deckle edge before you decorate the card, particularly if you are using this technique, as the water may ruin the decoration.*

---

15 Perforating edges

It's easy to create beautiful and delicate edges using a sewing machine with no thread to make perforations. Many machines offer a range of fancy stitches that work well. The perforated edge can either be left as a line of decorative holes, or torn away to produce a shaped edge.

1 Set a sewing machine to the required stitch. Place the card under the presser foot, a little way in from the edge, and stitch along. Use a guideline on the plate to help you keep the card straight. The perforations make a decorative pattern along the edge.

1

2 You can tear the card away along the stitched line so that the perforated decoration forms a new edge. Hold the card firmly and carefully pull the excess strip away. Pull a little at a time and move your fingers and thumb down the strip as you go.

2

◁ *Once you have made the perforations you can leave them as a decorative line running close to the edge of the card (far left). If you tear along the perforations you can create delicate and lacy edges that belie the ease with which they are achieved (left).*

Ideas & inspiration
Experiment with adjusting the width and length of the stitch to change its appearance. Scallop stitches usually make interesting perforated edges (top), and work well for torn edges, too (below). However, if the holes are too close together you will cut through the card, not just perforate it.

16 Hand-stitching edges

You can use many different embroidery stitches to decorate the edge of a card, consult an embroidery book and experiment with a few. A basic whip stitch is one of the simplest ways to decorate an edge and it provides a good basis for further embellishment with beads or sequins.

1 It is easier to make even, well-spaced stitches if you mark the card out before you start stitching. Decide how wide you want the border of stitching to be, then position a ruler on the card the required distance away from, but parallel to, the edge. Next, you need to consider how far apart you want the stitches to be. Use the ruler and a pencil to make evenly spaced marks down the edge of the card. If possible, try to make the stitches start and finish the same distance away from the top and bottom edges. In all the examples on this page the stitches are 10mm (½in) in from the edge and 15mm (¾in) apart.

2 Use a needle to pierce holes through the card where you made the pencil marks. Rub out the remaining pencil marks with a soft eraser.

3 Thread the needle with a piece of embroidery thread long enough to complete the line of stitching and knot one end. Bring it from back to front through the first hole at the top of the card and pull it through up to the knot.

4 To form the first stitch, take the thread over the edge of the card and bring it back up to the front through the second hole. Repeat all the way down.

5 Secure the thread on the back of the card at the end of the line of stitching. Take it under the last stitch, then pass the needle through the loop you have formed and pull it tight. Trim off the excess thread.

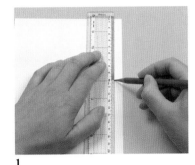
1

2

3

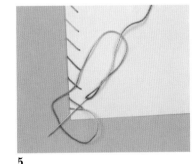
4

5

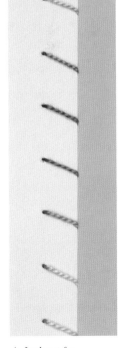

△ *Look out for multi-coloured threads or textured yarns to add further interest to the whip stitches.*

Ideas & inspiration

Once you have mastered the basic stitch there are many ways to develop the idea. Use very narrow ribbon threaded through small holes made with a paper punch (top).

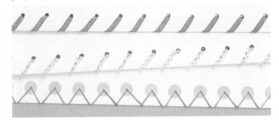

Beads can be strung onto thread before you start stitching (or bought ready-strung), and passed through punched holes (middle). If the beads are round, you can carefully punch the end holes slightly smaller than the beads, so that they can be pushed through quite snugly and hold themselves in place.

Sequins can also be threaded on as you stitch. Repeat the same stitch back along the edge of the card to hold the sequins in place (below).

17 Beading edges

Different stitches can be used in conjunction with beads to further embellish the edge of a card. Blanket stitch is great, as the beads can be applied on the horizontal or vertical part of the stitch and will therefore lie on the front or the edge of the card, as you prefer.

1 Mark out and pierce holes to stitch through as described in step 1 of *16 Hand-stitching edges* (see page 27). Thread a needle with a piece of embroidery thread long enough to complete the work, but don't knot the end. Working from the back to the front, bring the needle up through the top hole, leaving a long tail of thread at the back.

2 Push the needle through the second hole from front to back, but before pulling it tight, bring the needle around the edge of the card and through the loose stitch. To form the first full stitch, thread a bead onto a needle before pushing it through the next hole, from front to back. Again, don't pull it tight until you have brought the needle around the edge of the card and through the loose stitch, below the bead. The bead will sit on the vertical part of the stitch along the edge of the card. Repeat this until you reach the bottom of the card.

3 To keep the last bead in the correct position, finish by bringing the needle from back to front through the hole you have used to form the last stitch. Wrap the thread vertically around the bottom of the card and bring the needle back through the same hole. Wrap it round to the back of the work again and secure it as described in step 5 of *16 Hand-stitching edges* (see page 27).

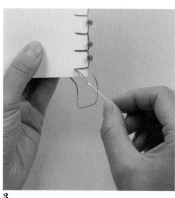

1

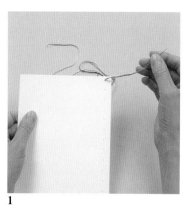

2

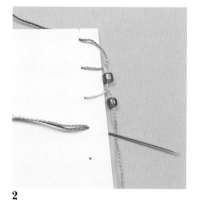

4

4 To finish off the edge neatly, you need to work the top to mirror the bottom of the line of stitching. Undo the first stitch

(the one without a bead) and thread the needle with the long tail of thread that you left. Thread a bead onto the needle.

Ideas & inspiration

Try using different beads in different positions. Varying numbers of small beads (top), or a long bugle bead (middle), can be threaded onto each stitch.

If you take the needle through the loop above the bead, rather than below it, the bead will sit on the front of the card, rather than on the edge of it (below).

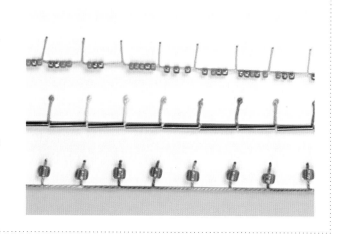

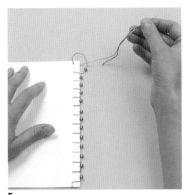

5

5 Take the needle through the end hole from front to back, around the card and through the loose stitch, above the bead.

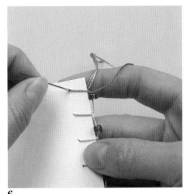

6

6 Anchor this beaded stitch by passing the needle through the same hole again, from back to front this time.

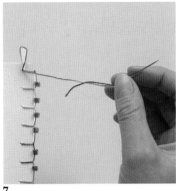

7

7 Finish off by wrapping the thread over the top edge of the card and securing it, as described in step 3.

△ *Keep the stitches fairly tight to ensure that the beads sit neatly along the edge of the card.*

18 Machine-stitching edges

Attractive stitched edges can be made using a sewing machine. Many machines are capable of a lot more than straight stitch or zigzag and it's well worth exploring the possibilities. It's vital that you test out the combination of stitch, thread and card before starting a project, as it's unlikely that you will be able to conceal any accidents.

1

1 Set a sewing machine to straight stitch at a tested length. Place the card under the presser foot, a little way in from the edge, and stitch along. Use a guideline on the plate to help you keep the card straight. Repeat the process a little further across the card to make two lines of stitching next to each other.

2 To prevent the ends of the stitching coming undone, knot them neatly on the back of the card before trimming off the excess thread.

2

◁ *To add yet another dimension to the edge, try using vari-coloured threads that subtly change shade as you stitch along.*

Ideas & inspiration

Some stitches, particularly zigzags, look better worked along the very edge of the card (first to fourth from top). To do this, position the card so that the needle comes down just off the edge of the card as you stitch along, going through the card on the left-hand side of the stitch only.

You can combine different stitches to create more complex and detailed variations. Try a line of scallop stitch bordered by or combined with straight stitch (fifth to seventh from top), or two lines of scallops overlapped to form a chain (eighth from top).

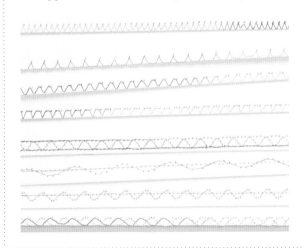

19 Colouring with a pencil

Colour applied to a deckle edge is fairly traditional and gives a classic look. There is a range of paper with coloured edges available commercially, but it's easy to do yourself and you can choose the precise colour you want.

1 Pencil a narrow line down the edge of the card with a watercolour pencil. Don't worry too much about keeping the line very straight or applying the colour really evenly, as the water will change things. Part of the charm of this look is a level of randomness.

2 Lift the card off the work surface and use a fine paintbrush to apply a little water over the colour. Avoid getting it too wet and brushing it too far out onto the card. Leave to dry.

1

2

Colouring techniques work well on straight or torn edges; it just depends on the look you want.

△ *On a straight edge, colour adds a decorative element.*

△ *The coloured strip highlights the unevenness of a torn edge.*

20 Colouring with an ink pad

This is a very simple, clean way of using ink to colour an edge, but almost any sort of media will work – watercolour paint, liquid ink or a brush pen. The effects will be slightly different, so it's advisable to test out the medium before starting a project. Dampening the edge of the card before applying the colour can give a softer result.

1

2

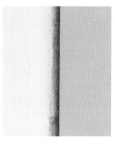

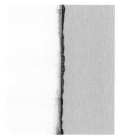

1 Dab a cosmetic sponge onto an ink pad to pick up a little colour.

2 With the card held away from the work surface and the sponge angled across the edge to be coloured, carefully rub the sponge along the card. Keeping the sponge at an angle helps to prevent the colour spreading too far onto the face of the card. Apply light pressure to the sponge at first and build up layers of colour gradually. Some inks come out looking stronger than you might expect.

△ *Careful application in layers allows you to build up a graduated band of colour along an edge.*

△ *On a torn edge the different textures of the paper will pick up the ink to different degrees.*

Getting it right
There are lots of ink pads in an enormous array of colours on the market and they are useful for many applications. Their biggest advantage is that they are mess-free and provide good, opaque colour.

Sticking and fixing

It is important to use an appropriate method of sticking and fixing for different elements on a card. Paper adhesive and a good all-purpose adhesive will solve most sticking issues, but check the label for suitability, and if you encounter problems, use a product specifically designed for the material. Always plan the layout of a card before applying adhesive to any of the elements. If the motif is to be centred and upright it is wise to pencil some light guidelines. Rub them out afterwards with a soft eraser. Excess or badly applied adhesive will ruin the look of a card, no matter how creative the design.

21 Paper adhesive

There are various paper adhesives available, but liquid gum-types can easily run out around the edges of your work, producing a messy result. It is best to go for drier, 'stickier' adhesives that will give a tidy result. The type of paper adhesive that comes in a stick applicator is ideal – clean and easy to use.

1 Place a paper motif face-down on scrap paper and apply a thin, even layer of adhesive to the back of it. The scrap paper allows you to spread the adhesive right over the edges.

2 Stick the glued motif to the card, positioning it carefully. Press it down to ensure that good contact is made. Leave to dry.

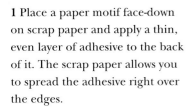

1

2

△ *Be careful not to transfer adhesive from your fingers onto the card or the surface will quickly become grubby.*

22 All-purpose adhesive

Although there are adhesives available for sticking specific materials, often a good, all-purpose adhesive will be adequate. All-purpose adhesive will stick a range of substances including paper, card, wood, leather, light metal, ceramic, shells and botanicals. Always consult the label, as many stronger adhesives will not be suitable for use on plastics, for example. Ideally, do a test first.

1 Apply adhesive to the back of a motif (here, a flower cut out of craft rubber), but not too thickly, particularly near the edge, or it may be forced out when you press the surfaces together.

2 Stick the motif to the card, positioning it carefully. Gently press down to ensure that good contact is made. Leave to dry.

1

2

△ *Gel-type all-purpose adhesive is easy to apply and doesn't tend to discolour or stain items over time.*

23 Glue pen

Adhesive is also available in handy pen-style applicators. The advantage of these is that they have fine tips, making them ideal for sticking on small embellishments like sequins. Often the adhesive is coloured on application and turns clear as it dries, making it easy to see while you are working.

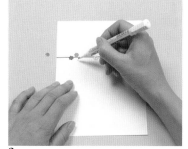

1 With a sequin face down on a work surface, or on the end of a dampened finger, apply a small dot of adhesive to the wrong side. Position the sequin on the card and leave it to dry.

2 It may be easier to apply a dot of adhesive onto the surface you are decorating and then lay the sequin onto that. You are more likely to stick things in exactly the right position with this method.

1

2

Getting it right
With small items, it is often easier to pick them up and position them on the dot of adhesive with the tip of a dampened cocktail stick (see *52 Embellishing a stamp*, page 53).

◁ *Use the pen to apply adhesive to a length of ribbon and stick it in place. Place the sequins on a dot of adhesive applied to the background.*

---

24 Fabric adhesive

If you are sticking fabric, then an adhesive specifically formulated for it is best. These tend to fall into two types, water-based or latex-based. Although latex-based adhesives are strong, they can discolour badly over time, so for most card-making activities the water-based sort is best. These are generally quite thick, white adhesives that dry clear.

1 Cut a piece of fabric to size and spread an even layer of adhesive onto the wrong side. Don't apply it too thickly, particularly near the edge, or it may be forced out and spoil the card when you press the surfaces together. If necessary, spread the adhesive thinly up to the edge of the fabric using a suitable tool. Leave it to dry until just tacky.

2 Place the fabric on the card in the required position and smooth it down with your fingers. Leave to dry completely.

1

2

◁ *Stick the gingham to the card and then stick on the printed fabric. Allow the first layer of fabric to dry before sticking on the second layer.*

Getting it right
If the fabric frays, iron fusible interfacing onto the back before you cut it out (see *67 Machine appliqué*, page 69). Fine fabrics may be unsuitable for use with adhesive, as it can show on the right side. Try hand or machine stitching these fabrics onto the card.

25 Masking tape

Masking tape is paper-based and compatible with many materials used in card making. There are special low-tack tapes available, but most types will peel off cleanly if you make a mistake. Available in a variety of widths, masking tape can be used to attach items temporarily or permanently, as long as it will eventually be concealed – because like all tape, it isn't very pretty.

1 A typical use for masking tape is in sticking a photograph, or other artwork, behind an aperture. Make a card (see *5 Three-panel cards*, page 18) and cut an aperture (see *6 Cutting square apertures*, page 18, and *7 Cutting shaped apertures*, page 20). Hold the aperture over the photograph and establish the area that will be visible within the opening. Trim the photograph to about 10mm (½in) bigger all round than the aperture. Place the trimmed photograph face-down and stick strips of masking tape across the top and bottom.

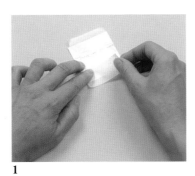

1

2

2 Turn the taped photograph face-up. Hold the card, right-side up, between both hands, just above the photograph. Move it around until the required section of the image is framed. Lower the card gently onto the photograph

until the tape touches the back. If it is not right, carefully peel the tape off and try again. When you are happy with the position of the image in the aperture, turn the card over and tape the other two sides of the photograph.

△ *Flat, thin artworks, such as photographs, are easy to stick into an aperture with masking tape. Thick artworks may present problems and alternative methods would be more suitable (see 98 Relief mounting, page 97, and 56 Running stitch, page 58).*

26 Double-sided tape

Double-sided tape is a most useful sticking and fixing material. It can be used on many surfaces where a neat, mess-free, but strong sticking method is required. It comes in different widths and you can also cut it to size with scissors. A typical use for double-sided tape is to seal the covering panel down on an aperture card (see 5 Three-panel cards, page 18).

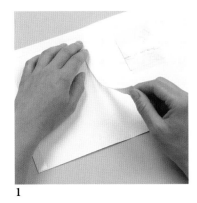

1

2

◁ *Double-sided tape works best on fairly thick paper or on card. On very thin paper it can show as a stripe on the front, so stick thin paper down with spray adhesive (see 29 Spray adhesive, page 35).*

1 Lay the card face-down and apply strips of double-sided tape close to each edge of the panel that will cover the back of the framed photograph, or artwork.

2 Peel the protective paper off the tape and fold the panel across to cover the photograph. Smooth the card down around the edges to ensure it is firmly stuck.

27 Double-sided film

Double-sided film is available in a variety of sheet sizes and has all the attributes of double-sided tape (see 26 Double-sided tape, page 33). It can be cut with scissors or a craft knife, paper punches or decorative-edge scissors and will stick many types of materials together. You can also use it to stick glitter, coloured sand, or accent beads in intricate shapes (see 22 All-purpose adhesive, page 31, and 95 Using glitter, page 94).

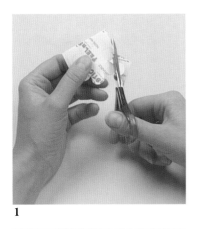

1

2

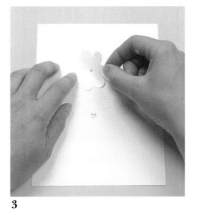

3

△ *Double-sided film is easy to apply, mess-free and very sticky, which means that fine sand and glitter stick evenly to it.*

4

5

6

7

1 Cut a motif out of double-sided film. You can do this freehand or cut around a transferred image (see *40 Transferring a template*, page 43). Use a shaped paper punch to cut some smaller motifs (see *75 Punching shapes*, page 76).

2 Peel the backing paper off one side of a motif. Do this carefully, especially with complex shapes, as it is possible to tear the layer of adhesive.

3 Position the motif on a card and press it down. Repeat with the rest of the motifs.

4 Decide which motifs are going to be decorated with sand and

peel the protective paper off these ones only to reveal the layer of adhesive.

5 Sprinkle the sand over the front of the card to cover the sticky shapes.

6 Lift the card up from the work surface, allowing the excess sand to fall off. Do this over a piece of scrap paper, which can then be used to tip the sand back into its container to be used again.

7 To complete the design, peel the protective paper off the remaining motifs and repeat the process with tiny accent beads.

28 Sticky mounting pads

Sticky mounting pads are available in different sizes and thicknesses to suit the item you are sticking. Made of foam, they are often used to create three-dimensional effects – you can even stack them up to give extra height. Here a purchased metal decoration is used to highlight a coloured sand flower.

1 Peel the backing paper off one side of a sticky mounting pad and stick it to the centre of the sand flower.

2 Peel the protective paper off the other side of the mounting pad. Stick the metal motif firmly onto it.

1

2

△ *The adhesive is fairly strong and because they are flexible, pads are useful for attaching inflexible items to flexible paper, forming a buffer between the two surfaces.*

29 Spray adhesive

Spray adhesive is multi-purpose and provides a permanent or temporary bond. It's fast-drying and translucent and you can apply a very sheer coat of adhesive to an item without touching it. Follow the manufacturer's instructions when using spray adhesive. The particles can drift, so ensure the work area is well-protected and ventilated; on a fine day, spray outdoors.

1 Place a panel and flowers cut from thin paper face-down on a well-protected work surface. Spray the adhesive on evenly from a distance of 150–200mm (6–8in). Excessive draft produced by the can may disturb or blow away the items you are trying to coat, so spray gently.

2 Lift the motifs up by the edges and stick them to the card. For the best results, cover the finished card with a sheet of paper for protection and roll over it with a brayer to ensure that the motifs are firmly stuck in place.

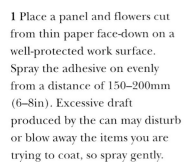
1

2

Getting it right

A brayer will come in handy when you are sticking, but it is a useful piece of kit to have for all kinds of tasks. It's a small, hardened-rubber roller, perfect for rolling over glued papers to ensure that they are securely stuck down. You can also use it to apply paint or printing ink directly onto paper or stamps.

◁ *Spray adhesive is indispensable for sticking thin paper and other lightweight or delicate items that would otherwise be very hard to handle.*

30 Paper fasteners

Paper fasteners are another mess-free way to attach items to a card. As they attach the item to the card at one point only, they allow movement to be introduced if desired. If you are worried about the sharp prongs, use a three-panel card (see 5 Three-panel cards, page 18), or cover the back with a panel, (see 6 Cutting square apertures, page 18).

1

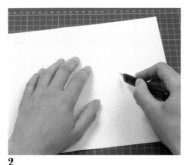

2

3

△ *The paper fastener forms the centre of the flower and the petals can rotate around it.*

1 Cut out some paper flowers and punch a hole in the centre of each one. To allow the flowers to rotate, the hole needs to be a bit larger than the width of a paper fastener's prongs.

2 Place the flowers on the card and mark the centre of each one. Open the card out flat and use a craft knife to cut a small slit in the card at each marked point.

3 With the card face-up, position the flower shapes over the slits in the card. Push a fastener through the centre of the flower and through the slit in the card. Turn the card over and open out the fastener's prongs.

---

31 Eyelets

Eyelets can be used to thread things through, but they can also provide an understated and contemporary fixing detail. Simple to apply through paper or cloth, eyelets come in different finishes and are available in small kits from good haberdasheries and craft stores.

1

2

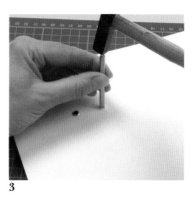

3

△ *To finish the design, knot a length of leather thong through the eyelets.*

1 Cut a flower from card and mark the positions of two eyelets with a pencil. Open the card flat on a cutting mat and position the flower. With a hammer and an eyelet tool, make holes at the

marked points. You can use paper adhesive to hold the flower in place while you hammer.

2 Push an eyelet into each hole from the front.

3 Lay the card face-down on a cutting mat. Position the tool on the eyelet and hammer the claws open. Remove the tool and hammer directly onto the eyelet to ensure that the claws are flat.

32 Rivets

Rivets are small two-part metal fixings, like those used on the pocket corners of jeans. You will find kits in good haberdasheries and craft stores. Although you could use adhesive, rivets are a neat way to attach thick or hard materials – such as denim, leather or rubber – to a card. Be sure to read the instructions on the kit carefully before you start.

1

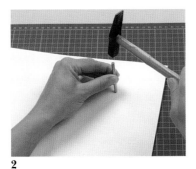

2

3

△ *The card and fabrics you use must be quite thick so that the rivet can grip the various layers firmly together.*

1 Cut a square of heavy cotton fabric and a flower out of leather. Position the flower on the fabric and use a leather punch to make a hole in the centre. (If there is a hole-making tool with the rivet kit, then use that instead.)

2 Lay the card flat on a cutting mat and position the square on it. Make a pencil mark on the card through the central hole. Use the tool and a hammer to make a hole through the card at the marked point.

3 Position the patch and flower over the hole and, from the back, pass the rear section of a rivet through the hole. Push the front section onto the back section. Hammer the rivet head until the patch is held tightly to the card.

33 Fusible webbing

If you need to need to join fabrics, or even wood veneers, together it's not necessary to use adhesive. Instead, buy some iron-on fusible webbing from a good haberdashery or craft store. This no-sew, paper-backed adhesive web is applied with an iron and allows you to bond fabrics together quickly and easily. It will also prevent the raw edges of fabrics from fraying.

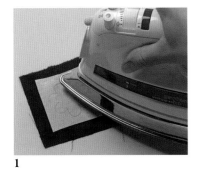

1

2

3

△ *Arrange all the motifs in position and iron them on in one go rather than separately, as each time you iron the card you risk the heat damaging it. If you are worried about this, join all the motifs with fusible webbing, then glue them to the card.*

1 Trace or draw a motif onto the paper side of a square of fusible webbing. Place the adhesive-coated side on the wrong side of the fabric. Dry iron it for about 5 seconds to transfer the adhesive from the paper to the fabric.

2 The fabric must be larger than the piece of webbing or you will stick the webbing to the ironing board. Cut out the motif with scissors and peel off the backing paper.

3 Place the motifs in position, adhesive side down, and cover them with a piece of baking parchment. Iron the parchment for a few seconds to bond the motifs together and to the card.

Decorating paper

Whether a decorated paper forms the main design of a card, or is a background for other elements, it's possible to achieve some unusual and exciting effects. There are hundreds of quick and easy ways to decorate paper and it's worth experimenting, as often an unplanned outcome can be most effective. The techniques shown here use a range of easily obtained materials: inks and domestic items you may have. Although the methods can be repeated, the results will never be the same. You can use these techniques to decorate large pieces of paper to use as gift wrap or to cut down to make cards, or panels for cards.

34 Colourwashing with ink

This is known as a 'wet-into-wet' technique, where the reaction between water and ink produces the result, and you have limited control once the ink is on the wet paper. If necessary, decant the inks into small containers before you start, diluting them with water if required. You will often find that diluting the ink does not noticeably compromise the strength of the colour, making this an economical medium.

1 Protect the work surface with paper or plastic, as this technique can be a bit messy. Use a wide paintbrush to brush water over the surface of a piece of watercolour paper. The amount of water you use and the length of time you leave it before applying the colour, combined with the absorbency of the paper, will all affect the outcome.

1

2 Using the wide paintbrush, brush lines of the first colour of ink across the paper, spacing them well apart.

3 Repeat the process in between these lines with a contrasting coloured ink to create stripes. Leave to dry completely.

2

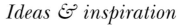

▷ *Use these decorating paper techniques for single-fold cards (see 4 Single-fold cards, page 17) and three-panel concertina cards (see 5 Three-panel cards, page 18), where the design will run across the whole face of the card. In both cases, it's generally best to decorate the paper before scoring and folding it.*

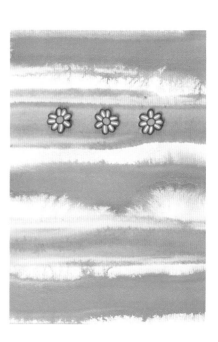

Getting it right

The water and ink mean that the paper is likely to distort slightly. Using a heavier-weight paper and avoiding over-wetting it can help. You can always press the paper flat again once it is dry by placing it under a pile of heavy books overnight.

3

Ideas & inspiration

Artist's inks are a great medium. They can be mixed or diluted and come in a wide range of colours, including pearlized tints. Most of them are transparent and as they are water-resistant when dry, you could try layering colours over each other to produce interesting mixes and combinations.

35 Dripping ink

Another wet-into-wet technique, this method requires no artistic ability at all. What's more, if you buy inks that come in dropper bottles you don't even have to dirty a paintbrush. It's fun to watch the patterns appearing like magic before your eyes.

1 Wet a piece of paper as described in step 1 of *34 Colourwashing with ink* (see page 38). Hold an applicator (a dropper or a paintbrush) a little way above the surface of the wet paper and move it around, allowing the ink to drip onto the paper. Leave spaces for dripping a second colour of ink.

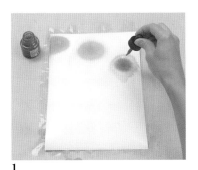

1

2 Repeat the process using the second colour. The colours will continue to blend and merge as long as the paper is damp. The final effect is only reached once the paper is completely dry.

2

Ideas & inspiration

You can create less random patterns by dripping the ink onto the wet paper in a more ordered way. These samples (below) were done on thick, absorbent blotting paper, which gives a lovely felt-like look to the final result.

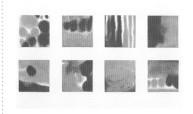

△ *As the decorated surface is quite busy, an applied decoration may get visually lost. To avoid this, mount the decoration onto a piece of plain coloured paper and then mount that on the card.*

---

36 Bleaching

This technique removes colour from paper rather than adding it. It works best on uncoated papers, but you can't tell how a paper will react just by looking at it, so it's best to test it – the effect should be almost instantaneous. Crêpe paper, sugar paper and tissue paper generally work well. Be very careful when using bleach, as it's an irritant and can damage many surfaces.

Protect the work surface with a sheet of plastic covered with paper. Decant some bleach into a small container. Use a notched foam brush to apply undiluted bleach in lines across the paper, spaced well apart. Moisten the brush with enough bleach to make a stripe with one stroke, as it will be difficult to stop and start halfway through. Repeat the process, running the stripes in the opposite direction to form a plaid pattern. Leave to dry completely.

Ideas & inspiration

Co-ordinate a card (right) and gift wrap (below) by mounting a panel cut from bleached gift wrap onto the card.

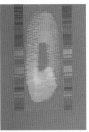

△ *This technique is particularly suitable for making gift wrap.*

Getting it right

Foam brushes are inexpensive, disposable and available in a range of widths. Cut notches along the edge so you can create a whole band of stripes in one stroke. Bleach doesn't damage foam, unlike hog's-hair brushes that quickly deteriorate. If you do use a paintbrush, try one with synthetic bristles.

37 Folding and dipping

This technique is based on a Japanese method of dying paper and cloth. The way the paper is folded and dipped has a big effect on the outcome: to create lines, dip the edges of the paper triangle into the ink and to create circles, dip the corners. It is best to use an uncoated, absorbent paper, such as mulberry paper. Practise on small sheets of the paper.

1 Fold a sheet of mulberry paper in half lengthways, aligning the edges.

2 Take the top layer only and fold it in half again, bringing it back across itself and aligning the edge against the first fold.

3 Turn the whole thing over and fold the second side back on itself in the same way. If you have done this correctly the fold formation will look like the inset picture.

4 Fold the top edge over and align it with the side edge to make a triangle. Make a firm crease to keep the triangle in place.

5 Turn the whole thing over and fold the first triangle over towards you.

Crease it into place. Turn the whole thing over again and fold the next triangle. Work your way to the bottom, turning and folding triangles.

6 If you are left with a short end of paper that isn't big enough to make another triangle from, trim it off with scissors.

7 Clamp the folds together with a bulldog clip. This also acts as a handle while you are dipping the paper.

8 Decant some ink into a small container and dilute it if required. Dip a point of the folded paper into the ink, allowing it to soak up the colour. Dip the remaining two corners into the ink in turn.

1

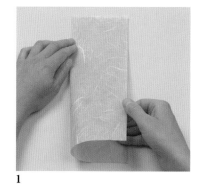
2

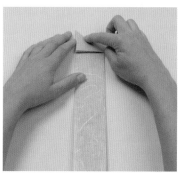
3

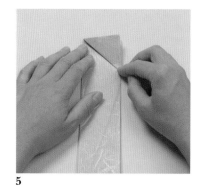
4

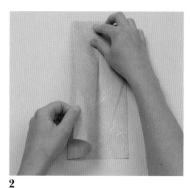
5

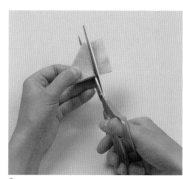
6

7

8

△ *Use this decorating technique to create your own gift wrap.*

9 Dip the edges of the folded paper into a different-coloured ink. You will have to move the bulldog clip round to allow you to dip the last edge.

10 Unfold the paper and allow it to dry completely.

9

10

Getting it right
Try experimenting with different, more complex folds and different-coloured papers. Make more intricate and layered patterns by repeating the process, either allowing the inks to dry between dippings, or re-dipping while they are still wet so that the colours blend.

Ideas & inspiration
You can make a greetings card to completely co-ordinate with a sheet of gift wrap that you have folded and dipped. Tear or cut out a panel of the decorated mulberry paper and use spray adhesive (see *29 Spray adhesive*, page 35) to mount it onto a card.

38 Wax resist

This is a very simple technique that demands nothing more than a white wax crayon – or a white candle – and some paper and ink. This is a great technique to do with a child, though it can be messy, so provide an apron and have paper towels standing by.

1

2

1 Protect the work surface with paper or plastic. Draw an all-over pattern on a piece of watercolour paper with a white wax crayon or household candle. If the paper is white, too, it's difficult to see the patterns you have made, so keep them simple.

2 Decant some ink into a small container and dilute it if required. Paint the ink over the surface of the paper with a wide paintbrush. Leave to dry completely. Press the dry paper under a pile of heavy books if the moisture distorts it.

Ideas & inspiration
Choose a defined area of the wax design to cut out and mount onto a card blank. You could also experiment with coloured crayons and coloured paper to produce a more complex effect.

△ *You can use the crayon or candle on its end or on its side to make thinner or thicker lines. This technique works well as a background for an applied decoration or motif, as the effect is quite subtle.*

39 Masking fluid

Available from art stores, masking fluid is a latex-based product that should never come into contact with your best paintbrush. Although it can easily be removed from watercolour paper, ideally within 24 hours, brushes will be ruined. Avoid using a paintbrush by buying masking fluid with a nozzle in the lid. This is good for mark-making and easy to use.

1 Protect the work surface with paper or plastic. Using masking fluid, draw bands of spirals across a piece of watercolour paper. Leave the fluid to dry.

2 Using a wide paintbrush, brush ink over alternate bands of the masking fluid pattern.

3 Repeat the process with a second colour of ink. Leave the ink to dry completely.

4 Use your fingertips to carefully rub away and peel off the masking fluid, revealing the original paper underneath.

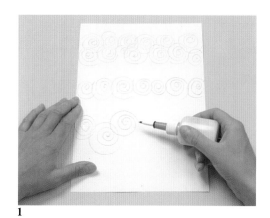

1

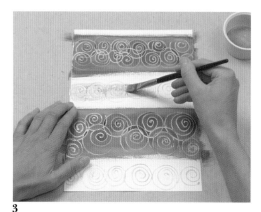

3

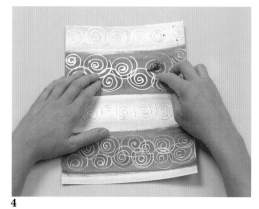

4

△ *You can create any patterns you wish with masking fluid. Apply a decoration with a complementary shape and colour to make the most of the pattern.*

Getting it right

The fluid is usually tinted, so you can see it clearly when you are working. Practise first on some scrap paper to get a feel for the speed you need to work at and and the flow control. If you make a mistake when creating a design, allow the fluid to set and then carefully peel it off the paper before you apply the ink.

Ideas & inspiration

Large sheets of decorated paper can be cut or torn up into small panels that can then be mounted on a card blank – an ideal way of producing a number of cards quickly and easily. You could also try using this technique on coloured paper, with a complementary rather than a contrasting coloured ink for a more subtle effect.

Transferring images

You will often want to use an exisiting image to decorate a card. It may be a design from the Templates section (see pages 154–158) transferred onto a card, or a purchased rub-down transfer from the huge selection available. You may want to use a found image, colour or black-and-white, on a card, but not on its existing background. This chapter assumes that you don't have a computer to reproduce images onto special transfer paper. The more manual methods described are particularly useful if you are using papers that won't work in a photocopier or printer, such as very fine or heavily textured papers.

40 Transferring a template

This technique is used to transfer an outline of a motif onto a card, to be cut out or worked on as needed. There are many techniques and projects in this book that require this technique. If the motif is not the right size, use a photocopier to enlarge or reduce it before transferring it.

1

2

3

4

5

1 Lay a piece of tracing paper over the top of a motif. If the motif is large or complex, tape the tracing paper lightly in position with masking tape to prevent it from moving about.

2 Trace the image accurately onto the tracing paper using a sharp, soft pencil.

3 Turn the traced image over and lay it face-down on scrap paper. Pencil over the whole image, using the side of the pencil lead.

4 Turn the tracing back over and lay it on the card in the required position. If necessary, tape the tracing paper in place. Carefully draw over the lines of the motif.

5 Lift the tracing paper off the card to reveal the transferred image. Proceed with the technique of your choice before removing the remaining pencil lines with a soft eraser.

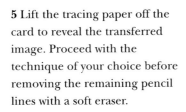

◁ *The pencil lines will be quite faint, but if necessary you can draw over them again in pencil.*

41 Image transfer paste

Image transfer paste will transfer any colour or black-and-white image onto fabric. Whether you choose a photograph or a printed picture, colour-photocopy it to the required size. The process reverses the image, so beware of using text or numbers. Full instructions are given with the product, so follow them carefully. This technique can't be rushed, but if you work the sequence through correctly, you will achieve a good result.

1 Cut out a colour photocopy with scissors. You can either cut immediately around the edge of the image or leave it on an area of background.

2 Place the image printed-side up on a piece of waxed paper. Squeeze on a generous amount of transfer paste and use a broad paintbrush to spread it fairly thickly over the whole image. You should be unable to see the image clearly.

3 Pick up the wet image carefully and place it on a piece of fabric, pasted-side down. Smooth the paper down gently to remove any wrinkles.

4 Place a paper towel over the whole image.

5 Lightly press the paper onto the fabric with a rolling pin or brayer, rolling in alternate directions. Continue until you are sure that the edges are stuck down.

6 Carefully remove the towel and use it to blot off any excess paste. Leave to dry for at least four hours, or ideally overnight.

7 When dry, place a wet sponge on the image and leave it for a few minutes, until the paper is thoroughly dampened.

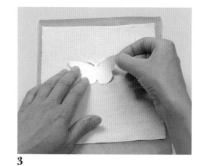

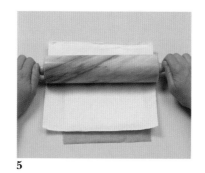

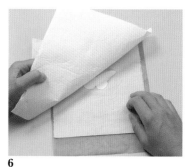

▷ *Cut the fabric to size or fray the edges (see 68 Fraying fabric, page 70), and mount it onto a card.*

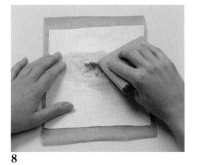

8

9

8 Using the sponge, rub gently in the centre of the image until the layer of wet paper comes off. Work from the centre out to avoid damaging the edges. Soak and rub until all the paper is removed. Leave to dry completely.

9 Squeeze a few drops of transfer paste onto the image and rub it gently into the fabric with a paintbrush. Ensure that the entire image is sealed in this way. Leave to dry completely.

Ideas & inspiration

Transfer a favourite photograph onto fabric to create a personalized greetings card and a long-lived memento of a special day. Choose a fabric to complement the picture; simple calico for a country walk, or white silk for a wedding photograph, for example. The paste only works on photocopies, it will just ruin an original photograph and not transfer the image.

42 Rub-down transfers

Available from suppliers of art materials, these transfers range from cross-sections of trees or vehicles, as used by architects, to letters in many different type styles. The computer has replaced the need for transfers in many applications, but they are great for card making. Letters and numbers are particularly useful, avoiding the difficulty of drawing them freehand.

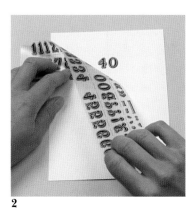

1

2

◁ *Use numbers to make a card for a significant birthday or anniversary.*

1 Use a set square and pencil to lightly mark guidelines on the card. Move a transfer sheet across the card until the number you require is in the right position. The backing paper is transparent, so you can see exactly what you are doing. Transfer the number to the card by rubbing the backing paper evenly with a tool; a dried-up ballpoint pen is ideal. It's important to apply even pressure to avoid the transfer cracking and producing a broken result.

2 Carefully peel the backing paper away to reveal the transfer. To ensure that it is fully adhered, place the piece of non-stick paper the transfer sheet was attached to on top of the number and burnish the transfer with a smooth-surfaced tool; a bone folder or the back of a teaspoon is ideal. Repeat the process for each number.

Ideas & inspiration

Create personalized greetings cards by using the name or initial of the recipient as the focus of the design. Rub the transfers down onto a panel of coloured paper and stick the panel to the card with paper adhesive (see *21 Paper adhesive*, page 31) or spray adhesive (see *29 Spray adhesive*, page 35).

43 Photocopies and thinners

Cellulose thinners can be used to transfer a black-and-white photocopied or computer-generated image onto a card. The image will be reversed, unless you reverse the photocopy first. The paper, image density, time allowed for the thinners to soak in, tool, and pressure used will all have an effect on the end result. When using thinners always follow the manufacturer's instructions, as it can be harmful if used incorrectly.

1 Photocopy a motif and cut it out, leaving a border of paper around the edge to hold it by.

2 Turn the image over and use a cotton wool bud to apply cellulose thinners to the back of the image. Don't worry that you can't see the image, the paper will become translucent where you apply the thinners, allowing you to see it clearly. Don't flood the paper, just put on enough to soak through.

3 Position the image over the card before carefully lowering it into place. Do not move it at this stage or the transfer will be blurred.

4 Holding the photocopy down firmly, rub evenly over the image with the back of a teaspoon. Be sure to cover every area. If you are careful it's possible to check on progress by lifting up a corner, then laying it back down in the same place if more rubbing is required.

5 When the image is transferred, carefully lift off the original. You can sometimes repeat the process using the same photocopy, but the image will be fainter each time.

1

2

3

4

5

△ *The transferred image often comes out slightly less crisp than the original, so select the image carefully. Sharp, high-contrast woodcuts transfer successfully, but it's worth experimenting with softer images to achieve a more subtle result, or a slightly aged look that can be effective.*

Ideas & inspiration

Use this technique to apply images to different surfaces, such as cloth (above), rough-textured paper (right), or even metal foil or wood veneer. The transferred image may not be very crisp, but it will still look good and could provide interesting material for a collaged card (see pages 84–86).

Getting it right

If you want to use an image with either text or numbers you will need to have it reverse-photocopied. This function is available on some photocopiers. Alternatively, it is possible to reverse an image on any photocopier by copying it first onto an acetate sheet, then reversing the acetate sheet and copying the image onto paper.

If you are using found images, make sure they are copyright-free. Books of such images are available from specialist suppliers. These cover many subjects and are often produced in black and white.

Stencilling and printing

Stencilling is an ancient art – there are prehistoric stencils of hands in Spanish caves and the basic technique has not changed in the thousands of years since they were made. Printing is defined in the dictionary as 'a mark left on a surface by something that has been pressed against it'. Although there are many sophisticated printing techniques today, this basic principle for transferring colour from one surface to another still applies. The techniques in this chapter show that modest materials and equipment are no hindrance to creativity. A little imagination is all it takes.

44 Stencilling

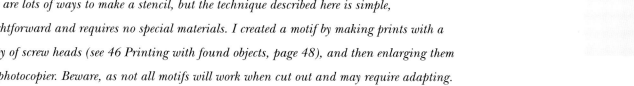

There are lots of ways to make a stencil, but the technique described here is simple, straightforward and requires no special materials. I created a motif by making prints with a variety of screw heads (see 46 Printing with found objects, page 48), and then enlarging them on a photocopier. Beware, as not all motifs will work when cut out and may require adapting.

1 Lay a sheet of tracing paper over a motif and trace it off using a sharp pencil.

2 Transfer the traced motif onto a piece of thin card (see *40 Transferring a template, page 43*).

3 Place the card on a cutting mat and carefully cut out the design with a craft knife.

4 Protect the work surface with scrap paper. Position the stencil on the card and holding it firmly in place, apply colour using a cosmetic sponge and an ink pad (see *20 Colouring with an ink pad, page 30*). Dab the sponge onto the ink pad, then dab the inked sponge over the stencil. Create shading by building up colour in some areas.

5 Carefully lift the stencil straight up off the card to reveal the final image.

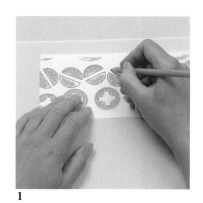
1

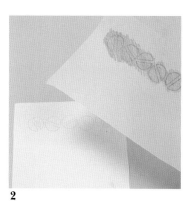
2

3

4

△ *Stamp pads are ideal for stencilling, as they produce strong, semi-dry colour that won't seep under the edge of the stencil card.*

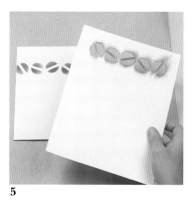
5

Getting it right

You can buy special stencil card in craft stores, but it isn't necessary unless you plan to use the stencil many times. A good alternative card is the kind used to make cereal boxes. This is thin but rigid enough and the glossy printing on the outside protects the card, to an extent, from the moisture of the ink.

45 Embellishing a stencil

Once you have stencilled a design you can add embellishments. There are lots of ways to do this – using a metallic pen or brush pen, applying glitter (see 95 Using glitter, page 94), sticking on gems or sequins (see 52 Embellishing a stamp, page 53), or using outliner and dimensional paint to give an area of the stencilled design a raised surface, as shown here.

1 Pipe a line around the edge of part of the stencilled design with glass-painting outliner. For best effect this should be done in one continuous movement. Practise first to ensure that the outliner is flowing well and to release any air bubbles. Leave to dry.

2 Fill the outlined shape with clear dimensional liquid. Leave to dry completely.

1

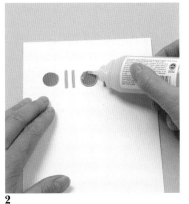

2

△ *If you can't find clear dimensional liquid in a craft store, then in this instance PVA adhesive would be a reasonable substitute. It will be white when you apply it, but as it dries it becomes clear.*

---

46 Printing with found objects

Printing with found objects can lead to interesting and surprising results, with no clues to the items that created them. Used in conjunction with distinctive papers, the abstract, printed outcome can be quite masculine, making it ideal for cards for the men in your life.

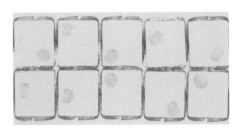

1 A multi-coloured ink pad offers a way of using several different colours easily and quickly. Press the back of a coat hook across the pad, so that it picks up more than one colour, and immediately press it down onto the card. Repeat the process until you have printed all the shapes you require. Ensure that you press the hook onto the pad in the same position each time, or the colours will quickly start to blend.

2 Use a silver ink pad and a nail head to print additional detail and complete the design.

1

2

◁ *The back of a coat hook and a nail head make a repeat design with a retro 1970s flavour.*

Ideas & inspiration

Try working on printed or embossed papers as well as plain ones. Print details to enhance the existing pattern to make gift wrap (left) or a card panel (right).

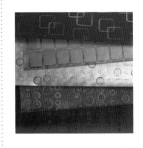
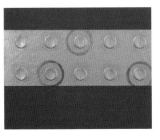

47 Mono-printing

This technique produces interesting, textural results, particularly if the process is repeated to create layers. The big advantage is that you can experiment on the piece of acetate before you make a print on the card. If you don't like the design, you can wash it off and start again. You can re-use the acetate many times.

1

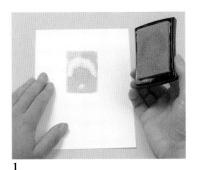

3

5

2

4

6

◁ *Try using different tools to make different marks in the paint; the wooden end of a paintbrush, or the rubber-tipped end of a pencil both work well.*

1 Make a coloured background for a mono-print by pressing an ink pad directly onto the surface of the card. Leave to dry.

2 Squeeze a little acrylic paint onto a sheet of acetate.

3 Use a pointed tool, such as a rubber-tipped paintbrush, to scribble lines into the paint, spreading it out across the acetate. Spread the paint out until it is approximately the same size as the ink pad print.

4 Position the acetate over the ink pad print, paint-side down, then lay it in place.

5 Smooth over the back of the acetate with your hand, ensuring that the acetate does not move and smudge the mono-print.

6 Carefully peel the acetate off the card to reveal the mono-print.

Ideas & inspiration

You can mono-print onto paper and cut or tear out a panel to mount on a card (right). This technique is also suitable for making gift wrap to match or complement a card (below). Make a matching gift tag as well for a completely co-ordinated greeting and gift (below right).

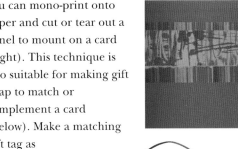

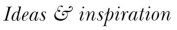

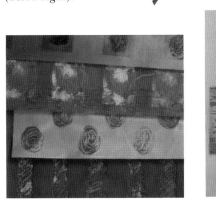

48 Potato printing

Almost all of us explore the potato print as a form of surface decoration when we are very young. Easy to use, cheap and readily available, the humble potato provides an excellent medium for creative expression. One of the simplest ways to produce repeat patterns, it's fast, satisfying and fun, and is a brilliant technique to use with children.

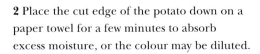

1 Cut a potato in half and draw the shape you want onto the surface with a soft pencil. Using a craft knife or sharp kitchen knife, carve out the shape carefully – children should not be allowed to do this. The shape to be printed should be approximately 5mm (¼in) higher than the surrounding potato. Simple shapes are easiest to do and you can build up more complex patterns from them by printing in layers and repeat patterns.

2 Place the cut edge of the potato down on a paper towel for a few minutes to absorb excess moisture, or the colour may be diluted.

3 Protect the work surface with scrap paper. Press the potato shape onto an ink pad and immediately press it onto the card, allowing some of the prints to run off the edge of the card for a more interesting effect. Repeat the process until you have printed all the shapes you require.

4 Repeat the process with a different shape and ink colour to build up a pattern.

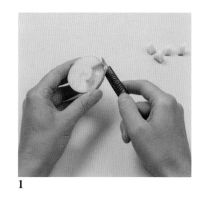

1

2

3

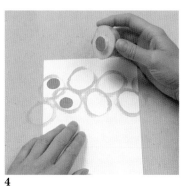

4

Ideas & inspiration

Select interesting papers and ink colours for a contemporary twist on an old technique. Printing techniques are well suited to making gift wrap, as they are easy and quick to do on a large scale (left). The printed paper can also be used to make a panel for a card that co-ordinates with the wrapping paper (right).

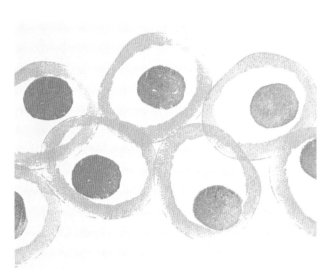

△ *This technique works well when applied straight onto the face of a card. However, if you are working with children, it might be best to stamp onto paper and cut out the best results to use as panels on cards.*

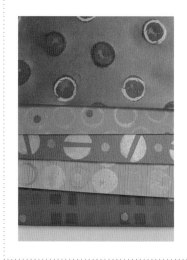

Spraying and stamping

Spraying and stamping techniques can produce effective results, fast. They are particularly useful for decorating large pieces of paper to be used as gift wrap, or to be cut down to make panels for cards. Alternatively, a stamped or sprayed detail could be the focus of a design, further embellished with added decorations such as sequins, gems or dimensional paint. Try using these techniques in conjunction with others, stamping on decorated papers, for example (see *Decorating paper*, pages 38–42) or spraying backgrounds to be stencilled or printed on (see *Stencilling and printing*, pages 47–50).

49 Silhouette spraying

Many items can be sprayed over, as long as they can be kept in place with low-tack spray adhesive (see 29 Spray adhesive, page 35), or are heavy enough to stay still while you spray – try keys, nappy pins, washers, shells or leaves. Open-weave fabric or lace can create interesting decoration. Don't use anything too precious, as it will get covered in paint.

1 To prevent spray paint from spreading onto the card, cut a mask the size of the card with an aperture the shape you want the sprayed area to be. Use a pencil and ruler to draw out the mask, then cut it out carefully with a steel rule and craft knife.

1

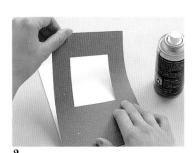
2

△ *If you are using a botanical it is better to use one that has been dried and pressed, as it will give a cleaner, crisper silhouette.*

2 Using low-tack spray adhesive, stick the mask to the card.

3 Within the masked area lay out some pressed fern leaves. When you are happy with the arrangement, stick the fern leaves in position with low-tack spray adhesive.

3

4

4 Protect the work surface with scrap paper and, following the safety instructions on the can, spray over the leaves and mask with stencil spray paint. Spray in short, light bursts to apply the colour evenly.

5

5 Before the paint is completely dry, carefully peel off the mask and then the leaves. You may find it easier to lift the corners of the leaves with the tip of a craft knife and then peel them back with your fingers.

Getting it right
It is important to stick the leaves down completely to prevent them from flying off the paper when you spray over them and to stop paint from bleeding under the edges and blurring the silhouette.

Ideas & inspiration

You can produce many different effects using the same principle. Try masking off half of the leaves at a time with scrap paper and spraying each half with a different coloured paint (top).

You can also stick the leaves to coloured or patterned papers, in this case a piece of an old map, before spraying over them (below).

50 Masking and spraying

Interesting effects can be achieved with spray paint and a shaped mask. The mask covers the background while paint is applied, producing a design when the mask is removed. You can quickly create a striped background for a card using tape as a mask. Tear the tape to give the stripes a broken edge. Protect the work surface with scrap paper, as spray paint can travel.

1

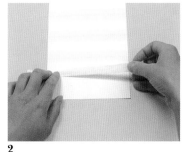

2

3

△ *The paints are quite opaque, so you can use a paler colour to spray the stencil and the stripes won't show through.*

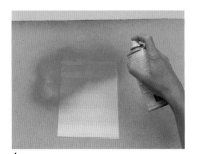

4

5

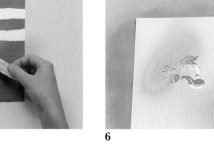

6

7

1 Cut a strip of masking tape slightly longer than the card is wide and carefully tear it in half. The two pieces will be used to form a single stripe, with the straight edges butted together on the card.

2 Before you apply the tape to the card, roughly work out the positions of the stripes, they should be evenly spaced. You can do this by eye, or measure if you prefer. Stick the first piece of tape right across the card.

3 Stick the second piece of torn tape next to the first, with the straight edges just overlapping. Repeat with more strips of tape until you have made all the stripes you need. Use scissors to trim off the masking tape protruding over the sides of the card.

4 Following the safety instructions on the can, spray evenly across the surface of the card with spray paint. Spray in short, light bursts to apply the colour evenly.

5 Peel the masking tape carefully off the front of the card to reveal the striped design. It is usually better to do this before the paint is totally dry.

6 Spray a design through a stencil over the stripes (see *44 Stencilling*, page 47). The stencil card should cover all of the

striped card, so that only the cut-out design is coloured when you spray. Use low-tack spray adhesive (see *29 Spray adhesive*, page 35) to hold the stencil in place.

7 Lift the stencil off the card to reveal the finished design.

Ideas & inspiration

Reverse the effect by masking off the leaf shapes rather than stencilling them on top. Stick cut-out leaf shapes to the surface of a card with low-tack spray adhesive. Mask a border either side of the leaves with torn tape and scrap paper before spraying the paint.

51 Simple stamping

Stamping is one of the easiest and quickest ways to decorate a card, especially if you use a ready-made stamp, of which there are lots on the market. Made of different materials, there are highly detailed rubber stamps, or more basic foam stamps such as the one used here, which was inexpensive and double-sided, giving two motifs to choose from.

1 To add interest to a stamped motif, use two shades of emulsion paint. Spoon them into a flat dish and, using the back of a teaspoon, spread them out quite thinly next to each other. The paints should cover an area slightly bigger than the stamp. Press the stamp face-down into the paint so that it is well coated.

2 Test the stamp on scrap paper. You may not need to apply paint every time, often the second stamp is best. To avoid mixing the colours, always put the stamp in the paint the same way round. When you are ready, position the stamp over the card and press down firmly, making sure that the stamp doesn't move and smudge the paint.

1

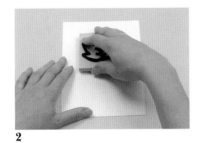

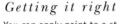

2

Ideas & inspiration

Stamp repeat images for gift wrap (right), or to make a panel for a card (below left). Try stamping onto interesting papers; leaf inclusions can be echoed with a stamped leaf motif (below right).

Getting it right
You can apply paint to a stamp with a paintbrush, but you must work quickly or the first colour will have dried before you have finished. If you are using one colour, you can apply the paint with a small foam roller.

◁ *The paper you stamp onto will effect the image; smooth paper will produce a clean stamp while textured paper will give a slightly broken, softer stamp.*

---

52 Embellishing a stamp

Stamps can be embellished in many ways; decorations can be stuck to them, as shown here; outliner and dimensional paint can be applied to them (see 45 Embellishing a stencil, page 48), as can embossing powder (see 91 Embossing with a stamp, page 90).

Stamp a motif onto a card and leave to dry. Dip the tip of a cocktail stick into all-purpose adhesive and dab a spot of adhesive onto the stamp. Damp the tip of a clean cocktail stick and use this to pick up a sequin and press it onto the adhesive.

Getting it right
You can also use a glue pen (see 23 Glue pen, page 32) to stick tiny items to a stamp.

◁ *Make the most of a stamped design by relief mounting it onto the face of a card (see 98 Relief mounting, page 97).*

53 Making a stamp from string

If you can't find a stamp with the design you want, make your own. This technique uses string to make an outline stamp, as opposed to a solid shape. There are many varieties and thicknesses of string and smoother types, like the parcel string used here, will give the cleanest outline. With care, the stamp should last well.

1

2

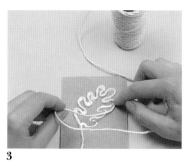

3

4

5

6

△ *Do not use different thicknesses of string on one stamp, or the thicker string will prevent the thinner string from touching the paper. Beware of using very thin string as it will be difficult to ink the stamp without getting colour on the background.*

1 Cut a piece of thin hardboard, or thick card, large enough to accommodate the motif. If you use hardboard, smooth the edges with fine sandpaper. Transfer a motif onto the hardboard (see *40 Transferring a template*, page 43).

2 Apply a line of fabric adhesive around the pencil outline.

3 Lay one continuous length of string along the line of adhesive. Butt the two ends together as neatly as possible. Leave to dry .

4 Apply silver ink to the top half of the stamp by rubbing an ink pad across it. This should minimize the amount of ink getting onto the hardboard and prevent the stamp from getting too wet. If ink does get onto the hardboard, wipe it off with a paper towel before you stamp, or it may transfer onto the card.

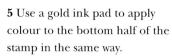

7

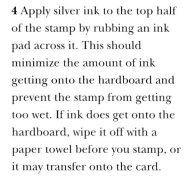

7

8

5 Use a gold ink pad to apply colour to the bottom half of the stamp in the same way.

6 Position the inked stamp over the card, then lower it onto the surface. Do not move the stamp or the image will be blurred.

7 Use a brayer to roll across the back of the stamp and ensure that all of the string comes into contact with the card.

8 Carefully lift the stamp clear of the card to reveal the image.

Ideas & inspiration

For a fresh look try stamping onto purchased, patterned gift wrap. This is a quick and effective way of producing a card panel (left) and co-ordinating, personalized gift wrap (right).

54 Making a stamp from sponge

Flat kitchen sponges are great for making stamps. They work best for solid shapes and the outline can be quite detailed. You can make line stamps from sponge, but if the lines are very fine, you will find it tricky to cut them out without breaking the sponge.

1 Transfer a motif onto the sponge (see *40 Transferring a template*, page 43). Pencil lines tend to rub away before you can cut the shape out, so draw over them carefully with a fine-tipped permanent pen.

2 Using sharp scissors, cut the motif out.

3 Carefully cut out the middle parts of the motif, using the points of the scissors to cut the fine detail.

4 Apply all-purpose adhesive to one side of the cut-out motif. Apply the adhesive evenly and right up to the edges.

5 Place the glued motif in position on a piece of hardboard or thick card (see *53 Making a stamp from string*, page 54).

6 Use a paintbrush to paint emulsion paint onto the sponge. It's important to keep the hardboard clean, so wipe away any excess paint with a paper towel as you work.

7 Position the stamp over the card, then gently lower it onto the surface. Do not allow the stamp to move or the image will be blurred. Use a brayer to roll across the back of the stamp to ensure that all of it comes into contact with the card.

8 Carefully lift the stamp clear of the card to reveal the design.

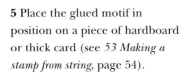
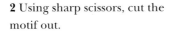
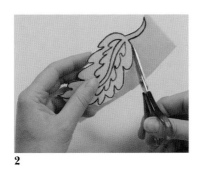

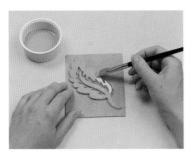
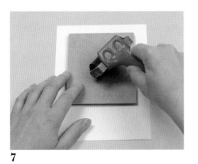
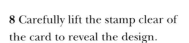
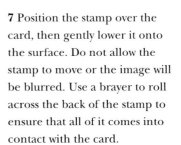

1

2

3

4

5

6

7

8

△ *The flat un-textured type of sponge used here produces the cleanest stamp, though the cellulose type will work, creating a more textured, uneven finish.*

Ideas & inspiration

Stamp a repeat design on coloured paper to make your own gift wrap (left). Making a matching gift tag is easy, too. Stamp a single design onto a piece of heavier paper, punch a hole and use co-ordinating embroidery thread to attach the tag to the parcel (right).

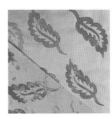

Stitching

Although stitching is usually thought of in conjunction with fabric, it works really well in card making, too, and offers lots of interesting possibilities. Use stitches individually as the focal point of a card, or combine them with other techniques to make more elaborate creations. Most of the techniques can be used on fabric that is then mounted onto a card, or you can work them directly onto the card itself. Look for unusual threads and yarns, the vari-coloured type that change shade as you stitch along are among my favourites. Always make sure that the thread you use is long enough to complete all of the stitching.

55 Simple straight stitches

You don't have to be an expert seamstress to create some interesting effects using hand stitches. Simple straight stitches worked in multi-coloured thread can be spaced either evenly or randomly to good effect.

1 It always helps to mark some guidelines on the back of your card before you start stitching. For evenly spaced, parallel stitches, draw two parallel lines across the back of the face of the card. Measure and mark out the positions of the tops and bottoms of the stitches.

2 Push a needle through the card at each marked point, so that you will be able to stitch from both sides of the card.

3 Thread the needle with a length of embroidery thread – double it if it is fine thread – and tie a knot close to the end. Push the needle through the first hole on the marked side of the card and pull it through up to the knot.

4 Make stitches through the pre-pierced holes, working from the front to the back of the card. On the back the stitches will be slanted and on the front they will form straight lines.

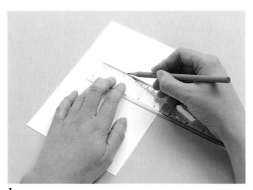

1

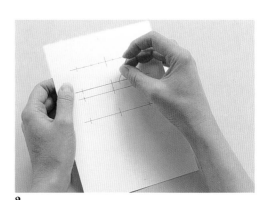

2

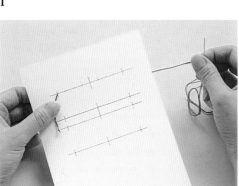

3

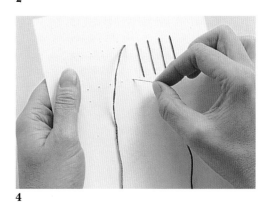

4

Getting it right

With all stitching techniques, consider how the whole finished card will look. If you are stitching fabric to be mounted onto a card and the edges are untidy, window-mount it in aperture (see *6 Cutting square apertures*, page 18, and *7 Cutting shaped apertures*, page 20).

When using ribbons and braids, which have two neat edges, pass the cut ends through slits cut in the card and secure them with tape on the back. If you are working directly onto the card, you could be left with an untidy finish on the inside. In any of these instances, it may be best to use a three-panel card (see *5 Three-panel cards*, page 18) or a single-fold card with an internal sheet (see *8 Internal sheets*, page 21), so that the inside of the card is neat.

If you are using thick yarn to make hand stitches on card, punch a hole to thread it through. This will remove a small section of the card and give a better finish than if you pierce the card and pull the yarn through.

5 For randomly spaced stitches, draw two parallel lines, as shown in step 1, but it is enough to just mark the outer edges and the centre point of the area to be covered with stitches (the centre mark will help you balance the number of stitches across the card). Using the needle, pierce a hole at each outer corner. When stitching through from the unmarked side of the card, first make a hole with a needle in the desired position on the marked side. Then turn the card over and make the stitch.

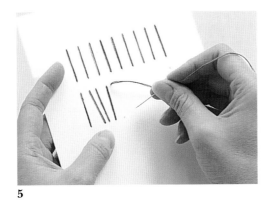

5

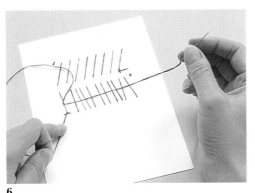

6

6 When you have finished, turn the card over and either loop the thread in a double knot around the adjacent stitch, or secure the end with a piece of masking tape.

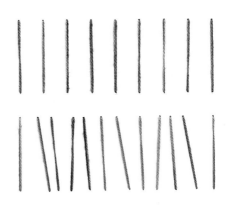

△ *Multi-coloured threads work well with simple stitches and used doubled they are even more colourful.*

Ideas & inspiration

As well as being decorative in their own right, straight stitches can also form the basis for a host of decorative applications. Stitches can be used to attach beads by simply threading the beads onto some of the stitches as you make them (below).

A row of parallel stitches can form a framework for weaving paper or fabric (top right).

Make the stitches, then just weave the material in and out of them (see *70 Simple weaving*, page 71).

Alternatively, simply feed a strip of decorative fabric with frayed edges (see *68 Fraying fabric*, page 70) or a length of ribbon under all the stitches to hold it firmly in place on the card (below right).

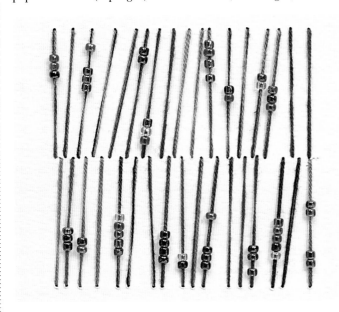

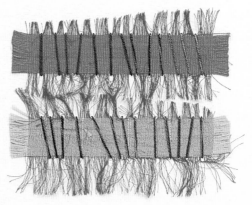

56 Running stitch

This is a simple and straightforward stitch that can be used as a decoration in its own right – try several lines running across a card next to each other. It's also useful as a method of attractively attaching a separate item to a card.

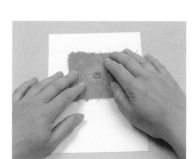

1 Tear a square of mulberry paper (see *13 Tearing against a rule*, page 25) large enough to accommodate both the decoration and the stitching that will be worked around it. Apply the decoration, in this case a pressed-flower sticker, to the square. To ensure the paper doesn't move while you stitch, apply paper adhesive to the back (see *21 Paper adhesive*, page 31).

2 Position the paper over the card and stick it down.

3 Use a needle to punch a hole through the card, from front to back, where you are going to start stitching. Thread the needle with a length of embroidery thread and tie a knot close to the end.

4 Bring the needle and thread through the punched hole, from back to front, pulling the thread through up to the knot. Push the needle back through the card and pull the thread taut to form the first stitch. Repeat the process to form a line of running stitches along the edge of the square. When you reach a corner continue stitching as before, changing direction on the back or front as necessary.

5 Stitch along each side of the square of paper. Make the final stitch and finish at the back by making a double knot over the first stitch you made, or securing the end with masking tape.

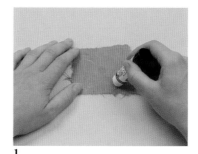
1

2

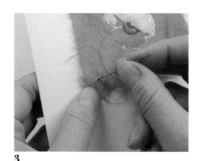
3

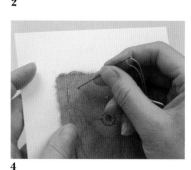
4

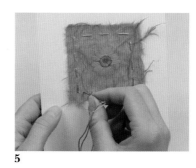
5

Getting it right

Work out roughly the number of stitches you can fit along one edge of the square in order to estimate the required stitch length. It doesn't matter if they are not all exactly the same length, but if you prefer you can measure and mark them.

Ideas & inspiration

Running stitch is very versatile and can be used in a number of ways. Attach ribbon to a card using running stitch to hold it in place and form a decorative edging (below).

Work lines of running stitch close together to form a motif (centre). Thread beads onto the stitches; try using beads of varying sizes (right).

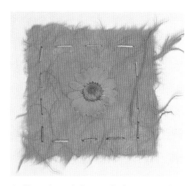

△ *Running stitches are both pretty and practical used in this way; they add detail and securely attach the main decoration to the card.*

57 Laced running stitch

This stitch is a simple development of plain running stitch (see *56 Running stitch, page 54*). A second length of thread or fine cord is passed up and down through the running stitch to sit on the surface of the fabric or card. Here the running stitch has been made using ribbon threaded in and out through a row of slits, allowing it to lie flat against the card.

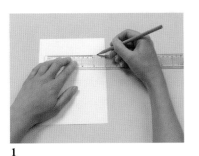

1

2

3

△ A fine cord (see *73 Making and using cord, page 74*) contrasts well with flat ribbon.

4

5

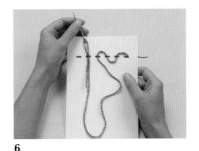

6

1 Using a ruler and pencil, draw a line across the card. There must be an even number of slits to ensure that the ribbon starts and ends on the back. Work out the positions of the slits; here they are 10mm (½in) apart. Mark the cutting points with a pencil.

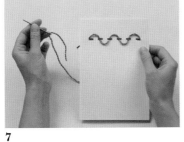

7

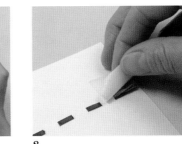

8

2 Place the card on a cutting mat. Use a craft knife to cut slits the width of the ribbon, working down from the pencil line. For narrow ribbon, make the cuts freehand; for wide ribbon, cut against a steel rule between two marked points. Rub out the pencil marks with a soft eraser.

3 Thread a needle with a length of ribbon and draw it through the first slit, from back to front. Leave a short end.

4 Pass the ribbon in and out of the slits, finishing on the wrong side and leaving a short end.

5 Thread the needle with a length of fine cord and pull it through the first slit, from back to front. Leave a short end, which will be taped down with the ribbon.

6 Pass the cord up and down through the ribbon stitches, forming even loops.

7 Finish by taking the cord through the last slit to the back.

8 Trim the ends of the cord and the ribbon, then stick them to the back of the card with masking tape.

Ideas & inspiration

Double the effect by threading strips of frayed fabric (see *68 Fraying fabric, page 70*) in and out of parallel rows of running stitch, twisting them round each other between stitches (right).

Decorate ribbon with lines of laced running stitch and tiny beads (below).

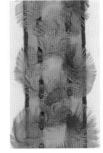

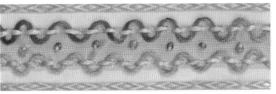

58 Lazy daisy stitch

A perennial favourite, lazy daisy stitch can look charming when applied directly onto the surface of a card. If you want the petals to look even and regular, it's best to mark their positions out first, as unlike cloth, the marks from any mistakes will remain visible.

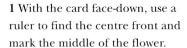

1 With the card face-down, use a ruler to find the centre front and mark the middle of the flower.

2 Use a compass positioned on this mark to draw two concentric circles to mark the inner and outer extremities of the flower. Here, the inner circle has a 5mm (¼in) radius and the outer circle a 15mm (¾in) radius.

3 Bisect the circle with horizontal and vertical lines through the centre point, then divide these sections in half again. If you are making a bigger flower you may need to divide the sections again.

4 Using a needle, pierce a hole at each point where the straight lines cross the circles.

5 The back of the prepared card should look like this.

6 Thread the needle with embroidery thread and tie a knot in one end. Turn the card over and bring the needle from back to front through one of the holes on the inner circle. Pull the thread through up to the knot.

7 Form the first petal by holding a loop of thread with your thumb, while you pass the needle back down through the hole it came out of.

8 Bring the needle back out to the front of the card through the opposite hole on the outer circle. Pass it through the loop of thread made in step 7.

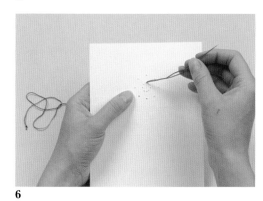

1

2

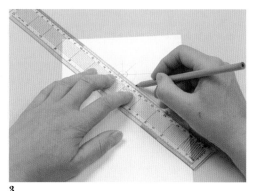

3

4

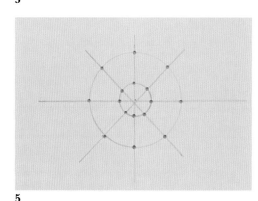

5

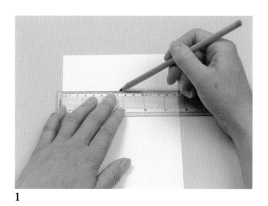

6

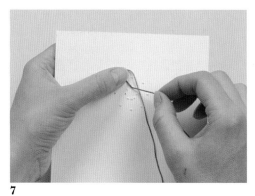

7

8

9 To complete the first petal, anchor the loop by passing the needle back down the hole in the outer circle that it came out of, creating a little holding stitch.

10 Repeat the technique, working between all the pairs of holes around the circle.

11 When all eight petals have been stitched, knot the thread on the back or stick it down with masking tape.

9

10

11

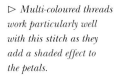
▷ *Multi-coloured threads work particularly well with this stitch as they add a shaded effect to the petals.*

Ideas & inspiration

Use wool to stitch flowers onto flat braid and whip stitch the edges for extra detail (above). Cut slits in the card, tuck the cut ends of the braid through them and tape the ends down at the back.

Applied more conventionally to fabric, the flowers can be embellished with beads (right). Mount the fabric onto the card with adhesive (see *24 Fabric adhesive*, page 32) or running stitch (see *56 Running stitch*, page 58).

59 Sheaf stitch

Like lazy daisy, sheaf stitch produces individual motifs that are decorative in their own right and a few stitches can take centre stage on a card. For the best effect it's worth testing out the stitch in the thread you intend to use in order to work out the optimum stitch spacing and height.

1 Working on the back of the card, measure and draw three evenly spaced, parallel lines across the card; here the two outer lines are 15mm (⅜in) apart. Find the centre of the card and mark a set of three holes on the top line and another parallel set on the bottom line. Mark a single hole on the middle line, aligned with the centre hole on the top and bottom lines. Mark the positions of more sets of holes on either side of the centre set until you have as many sets as you want. Here there are five sets, spaced 15mm (⅜in) apart.

2 Use a needle to pierce holes at the marked points. This will allow you to form the stitch accurately from the front or back of the card.

3 Thread the needle with embroidery thread and make a knot in the end. Turn the card over and bring the needle from back

to front through the top left hole. Draw the thread through up to the knot.

4 Form the first upright by pushing the needle from front to back through the bottom left hole. Pull the stitch taut. Bring the needle back through the adjacent hole to the right. Form the next upright from bottom to top, passing the needle back through the hole in the top line above the one it came out of. Form the last of the three upright stitches from top to bottom, bringing the needle through the next hole to the right and back through the bottom right hole.

5 Bring the thread through the hole in the centre of the uprights. Loop the thread around the three upright stitches, then take the needle back through the same hole and pull the thread taut. This will gather the uprights together in the centre to 'tie' the sheaf.

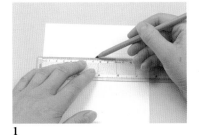
1

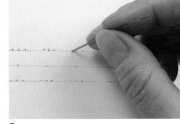
2

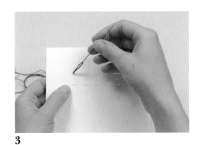
3

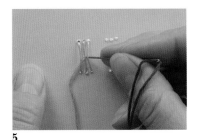
4

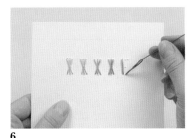
5

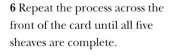

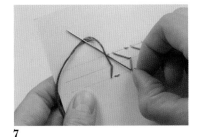
6

6 Repeat the process across the front of the card until all five sheaves are complete.

7 Finish by knotting the thread on the back of the card and trimming off any excess.

7

Ideas & inspiration

Coloured string is used to make tall sheaves that are decorated with a bead threaded on as the 'tie' is formed (right).

Arrange sheaves in a pattern using checked fabric or ribbon as a guide (far right). Multi-coloured thread adds extra interest.

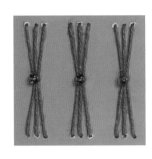

△ *Embroidery thread in graduated shades of pink is used to make these sheaves. The spacing of the stitches means that the sheaves change colour across the card.*

60 Using beads

There are some beautiful beads available that can be used as the main feature of a card, as here, or strung to form an edge (see 17 Beading edges, page 28). Look out for lovely old beads in second-hand shops and give them a new lease of life by working them into card designs.

1 The beads will dangle from three points spaced across the card, so mark these positions first. Here, they are 25mm (1in) apart.

2 Use a beading needle to pierce holes at the marked points. Thread the needle, ideally with special beading thread for strength.

3 Pass the threaded needle through the centre hole from the back to the front. Leave a long end and secure it temporarily with a piece of masking tape stuck just above the line of holes.

4 Thread the beads onto the needle, ending with a larger bead. Push the beads up the thread until they sit against the hole.

5 Bypassing the larger bead, thread the needle back up through the beads, then through the hole to the back of the card. Pull the thread gently to hold the top of the string of beads firmly against the card.

6 Bring the needle out through one of the remaining holes and repeat the process. Cross to the last hole and complete the final string of beads.

7 Carefully peel off the masking tape and bringing the ends of the thread together at the centre, tie them off securely. Replace the masking tape to cover the threads.

1

2

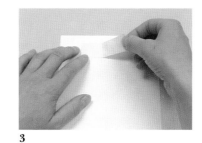

3

4

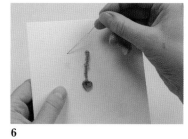

5

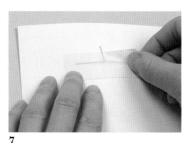

6

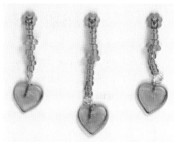

7

Ideas & inspiration

Use beads as an edging for an applied motif, stitched on individually or strung together to form looped sections (right). Embellish checked ribbon by stitching on an arrangement of beads and star sequins (far right). Combine different beads to make stamens for flower buttons (below).

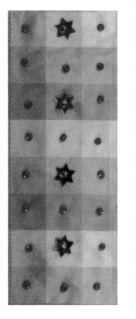

△ *Make the strings of beads different lengths and use different shaped and sized beads for the best effect.*

61 Using buttons

Like beads, there are many lovely buttons available. If you are really lucky, you may have grandma's button box tucked away, which is sure to contain some lovely old glass or engraved mother-of-pearl examples. Often you will have only two or three of each button, so using odd ones to decorate cards is a lovely way to make the best of them.

1 Use a pencil and ruler to mark a faint line across the front of the card. Make a mark at the centre of the line. Work out how far apart the buttons should be and mark the positions on either side of the central point. Here they are 25mm (1in) apart.

2 Position each button and mark through the holes with a sharp pencil.

3 Use a needle to pierce a hole at each marked point. Rub out the pencil marks with a soft eraser.

4 Thread the needle with embroidery thread and knot the end. Bring it through the first hole from back to front, pulling the thread through up to the knot.

5 Thread the needle through one hole in the button, then back through the second hole and through the appropriate hole in the card. Pull the thread gently so that the button sits flat against the card. Bring the thread up through the next hole and repeat the process until all the buttons are stitched on. Finish by making a double knot on the back and trimming excess thread.

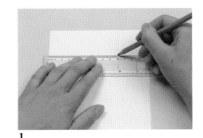
1

2

3

4

5

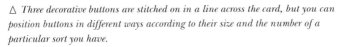

△ *Three decorative buttons are stitched on in a line across the card, but you can position buttons in different ways according to their size and the number of a particular sort you have.*

Ideas & inspiration

Stitch alternate buttons and sequins onto pieces of ribbon, adding tiny beads as you go (top). Cut slots in the card and tuck the cut ends of the ribbon into them, taping them at the back.

Stitch on a row of mother-of-pearl buttons in a less formal way. Here, the back of the buttons face out, showing off their textures and markings (centre).

Make use of worn-out shirts by cutting up sections of the front placket and buttoning them onto the front of a card (below).

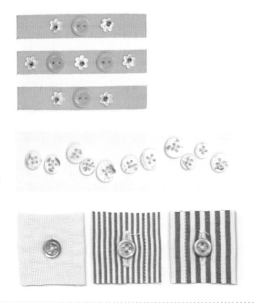

Almost any small item with a hole can be stitched to the front of a card. Keys, washers, charms, bits of jewellery – all can make interesting decorations. Keep likely objects together in a small container so they are easily found when you need them.

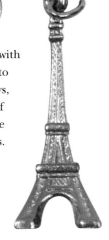

62 Using shells

Shells can be quite difficult to stick securely onto a greetings card with adhesive. An alternative is to stitch or tie them on, but this requires a small hole. Sometimes pre-drilled shells are available, but if you want to use shells you have collected, you need an electric hobby drill.

1 Make a small hole in each shell with an electric hobby drill. Having the drill on a fairly high speed, but going slowly and not applying too much pressure is usually the most effective method.

2 Place the shells in position on the card and make a pencil mark at the top of each one. Make another mark below the first ones to correspond with the position of the drilled hole. Use a needle to pierce holes at both marked points. Rub out the pencil marks with a soft eraser.

3 Thread a needle with a length of embroidery thread. To attach the first shell, pass the needle through the top hole from front to back, leaving a long end at the front. Bring the needle back through the lower hole.

4 Pass the needle through the hole in the shell from back to front, and then remove the needle.

5 Tie the shell to the card with a double knot.

6 Trim the threads, leaving short ends, and separate the strands for further decoration. Repeat the process to attach the second shell.

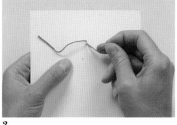

1

2

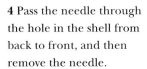

3

4

5

6

▷ *Tie two halves of the same shell to a card with co-ordinating embroidery thread.*

Getting it right

Drilling isn't difficult, but the fragility of the shells usually leads to some breakages. Start with more shells than you need and practise on a couple of less-beautiful ones.

Ideas & inspiration

Suspend a mussel shell from an organza bow. Tie the bow (see *72 Tying perfect bows*, page 73) and attach the drilled shell to it with a couple of stitches (top).

Drill holes in three cockleshells and fasten them to a card with natural raffia. Flecked card picks up their colours and textures (centre).

Stitch drilled mussel shells along the edge of ribbon or braid. Tuck the ends of the ribbon through slits cut in the card (below).

It's well worth considering whether other found items without holes could be drilled and used to decorate a card. Look at small pieces of slate, driftwood or bark, pre-cut wooden shapes, parts of models or toys, circuit boards and electrical components, clock or watch parts and old coins.

63 Simple machine stitching

Machine stitching can be used to create the main design element on a card. However, it's also a great way to attach items; it's often neater and easier than gluing and adds further decorative detail. Not all stitches are suitable for use on paper. If the stitch is too small you will over-perforate the paper, which will then simply fall apart.

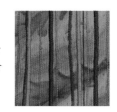

Cut a motif from fabric or paper. Position it on the card and hold it firmly in place while you stitch all the way around, close to the edge. Don't over-run at the corners and turn the corner with the needle down through the card to make nice sharp right angles. If you are worried about keeping the motif in position while you stitch, secure it with a dab of suitable adhesive. If the fabric is very fine, or likely to fray badly or distort in the sewing process, apply iron-on interfacing to the back before cutting the motif to size (see *67 Machine appliqué*, page 69).

△ *A square of printed cotton is stitched to this card, but it could be a motif cut from paper. Don't forget to test the stitch first to set the length correctly.*

Ideas & inspiration

Create stripes on fabric by setting the machine on a very close zigzag stitch. You can alter the stitch width to make wide or narrow stripes. Apply iron-on interfacing to the back of the fabric before sewing (right).

Decorate a paper panel with close lines of stitching and some sequin highlights (below).

---

64 Freehand machine stitching

This is a more advanced technique, where the sewing machine becomes a kind of drawing tool. It takes a little practice to become proficient in steering the fabric, but it is great fun and you don't need a lot of expertise to achieve good results. Look out for vibrant, vari-coloured and metallic machine-embroidery threads. Straight or zigzag stitch can usually be used, each giving a different look.

Some machines have a special embroidery foot that replaces the regular foot (check your sewing machine manual), but if your machine doesn't, you can usually work without a foot on at all. In all cases you need to drop the feed teeth located below the foot. Iron interfacing onto the back of the fabric (see *67 Machine appliqué*, page 69). The interfacing and an embroidery hoop should prevent the fabric from distorting too much. If necessary, mark out a design on the fabric using tailor's chalk. Fix the interfaced fabric into the embroidery hoop so that it will rest flat on the bed of the machine. Start to work the design, moving the hoop round as necessary with your fingers.

△ *Make a concentric circle motif, building it up with different colours of thread and ordinary straight stitch. Always test the stitch and machine settings before you start a project.*

Ideas & inspiration

Printed fabric can be worked into by filling in some areas or outlining them with freehand stitching. A marbled paper background is attached to the card with straight stitch.

65 Stitching acetate and plastic

Working with acetate or plastic offers exciting possibilities for making cards and attaching it with stitch avoids any of the untidy problems that would occur using adhesives. Transparent or semi-transparent plastic can be used to trap items, either protecting them or containing them. Use invisible thread when sewing plastic to preserve the transparent quality.

1 Cut a square of acetate, either plain or printed, and position it on a card. Holding it firmly in place, stitch it to the card, leaving an opening in the bottom edge.

2 Push some sequins under the open edge with your fingertip. Stitch the opening closed, overlapping a few of the stitches at either end through the previous stitching holes.

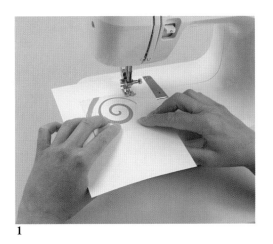

1

2

▷ *Use printed plastic to contain sequins, confetti or any other flat items. Acetate or plastic is usually interchangeable with transparent fabrics (see 69 Using transparent fabric, page 71).*

Ideas & inspiration

Try using coloured, printed plastic, the sort that florists use, to create some interesting effects. Trap confetti shapes mounted on plain card underneath a flower-printed plastic (right).

Many delicate natural forms can be protected and their beauty fully appreciated when they are trapped under acetate. It's a useful way to mount items such as downy feathers (far right), which would look ugly and lose their fluffiness if glued. Pressed flowers (below right) can be glued to a card (see *80 Attaching flowers and petals*, page 82), then acetate stitched over them to protect them.

Getting it right

Acetate can be slightly more difficult to sew than fabric, so practise before you begin a project. The other point to remember is that mistakes cannot be removed; make a line of holes in the wrong place with the sewing machine and there they stay. Whether you are stitching acetate, paper or fabric, spend time exploring and experimenting.

For other ideas using a sewing machine look at *15 Perforating edges* (see page 26), *18 Machine-stitching edges* (see page 29), *63 Simple machine stitching* (see page 66), *64 Freehand machine stitching* (see page 66), *67 Machine appliqué* (see page 69), *76 Piercing paper* (see page 76) and *78 Perforating* (see page 79).

66 Hand appliqué

Appliqué is usually thought of in the context of fabrics, but it can be successfully used to join fabric to paper or paper to paper. Try using fabrics with interesting surfaces to add texture to a card. If you are using lightweight fabrics or fabrics that fray easily, or to stop fabrics distorting, apply iron-on interfacing before you cut shapes out (see 67 Machine appliqué, page 69).

1 Cut a heart out of red felt. Measure and mark where it will sit on the card with a pencil. Apply a little fabric adhesive (see *24 Fabric adhesive*, page 32) to the wrong side of the heart, keeping it away from the edges.

2 Position the motif over the card and press it down.

3 Thread a needle with a length of yarn and knot the end. Use the needle to pierce a hole through the felt and the card from the front to indicate the starting position of the first stitch. This stitch will be made from the back, so the hole will ensure that it starts in the right place. Whenever you have to work from the back, pierce a hole from the front first, so all the stitches are planned and marked from the right side.

4 Pass the needle through the pierced hole, from back to front, and pull it through up to the knot.

5 Make the first stitch by pushing the needle back through the card, just off the edge of the felt. Pierce a hole for the second stitch from the front, and then bring the needle through it from the back of the card.

6 Repeat this process, working all around the edge of the motif and making the stitches deliberately uneven to create a naïve look.

7 Complete the final stitch and secure the yarn at the back by forming a double knot over an adjacent stitch.

1

2

3

4

5

6

7

◁ *This red felt heart outlined with pink woollen stitches is a good way to get the message across to your loved one. Since felt doesn't fray, and is reasonably thick, there is no need to apply interfacing to the back. The heart could be further embellished using beads, sequins or other embroidery stitches.*

Getting it right
It can be difficult to keep the motif in the correct position as you sew around it, so sticking the motif to the card with adhesive first is a good idea. You are then free to concentrate on the decorative quality of the stitches. Simple straight stitches have been used on this heart, though others, such as running stitch, could work, depending on the fabric.

67 Machine appliqué

Machine stitching gives a strong outline to appliquéd motifs and provided you have prepared the fabrics properly, is simple and quick to do. If you wish to apply fabric to fabric, it is best to bond them together first using fusible webbing (see 33 Fusible webbing, page 37). This resolves the problem of any movement or fraying and allows the stitch to be applied in a purely decorative capacity.

1 Apply iron-on interfacing to the wrong side of the background fabric. Always iron the interfacing onto the fabric before you cut it to size. Iron fusible webbing onto the back of a small piece of contrast fabric. Cut out a heart shape and bond it to the background with an iron.

2 Use an embroidery hoop while stitching if you are worried about the fabric distorting. Test the stitch on some scrap fabric. A wide, close zigzag, called satin stitch, works well. A more open zigzag, a fancy embroidery stitch, or straight stitch could be used if you prefer. Except for straight stitch, position the work so that the stitch will sit mostly on the motif, passing over onto the background approximately 2mm (⅛in) from the motif edge. Sew around the motif, working the stitch carefully around corners or intricate shapes. Finish by pulling the threads through to the back of the fabric and trimming off any excess.

3 Cut the background fabric to size with pinking shears. Position the fabric on the card, gluing it first if you prefer, and attach it to the card with straight stitch (see *63 Simple machine stitching*, page 66).

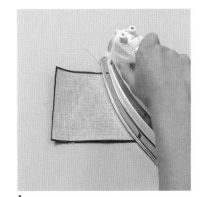

1

2

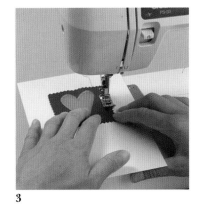

3

△ *This technique can make use of all sorts of small scraps, so suddenly the tiniest piece of fabric has creative potential. It can also make very expensive fabric go a long way. Collect a few pieces and store them together for future use.*

Ideas & inspiration

Cut out motifs from printed fabric, leaving a narrow border of background around the edge of each motif (below left). Appliqué the motifs to a contrasting fabric background, then stick or mount the panel onto a card (below right). Appliqué several images onto the same piece of background fabric for a more complex effect.

Getting it right

Available from fabric and craft stores, iron-on interfacing is fabric with a layer of adhesive on one side. There are a variety of types available – woven and non-woven; heavy-, medium- and light-weight. For most jobs, medium-weight, non-woven is fine. Cut the interfacing a little smaller than the main fabric, and always ensure that you place it on the wrong side of the main fabric, adhesive-side down, or you will be left with an awful mess on your iron and ironing board!

Fabric and ribbon

Textiles, in the forms of fabric, ribbon, braid, cord, thread, and so on, are a most versatile and exciting medium. There is an almost infinite range to choose from, much of which is inexpensive, especially in the tiny quantities needed for making cards. Whenever an interesting fabric or pretty cord catches your eye in a store, buy a little of it, it will come in useful. Keep pieces of favourite garments, scraps left over from sewing projects and ribbons and cords from packaging and store all these remnants in boxes – shoe boxes are ideal – so that you can find them easily when you need them.

68 Fraying fabric

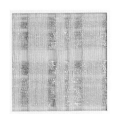

Many fabrics will fray if the edges are left untreated and this can be used as decorative detail on a card. However, there is a world of difference between deliberate fraying and fraying from poor handling or application. Woven fabrics fray on the straight grain, so you can't fray around a circle. Fraying along straight edges is usually a quick process, but will depend on the fabric.

1 To create straight, evenly frayed edges, the piece of fabric must be perfectly true to the grain. To establish this, first cut a piece of fabric slightly larger than you need.

2 Pull out a few warp and weft fibres until a whole thread pulls out right along the edge and you can clearly see the true, straight grain in both directions. Continue pulling out more threads until the fabric is the size you want.

3 Cut off the frayed edges so that you have a piece of perfectly true fabric that is exactly the right size.

4 Once again, pull out warp and weft threads, this time fraying the edges to the depth you require.

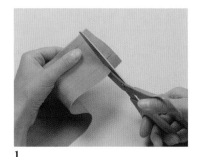
1

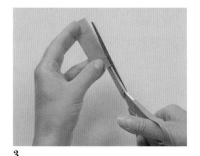
2

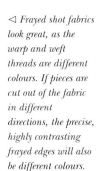
3

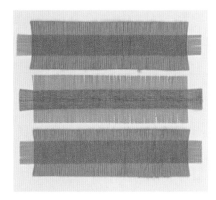
4

◁ *Frayed shot fabrics look great, as the warp and weft threads are different colours. If pieces are cut out of the fabric in different directions, the precise, highly contrasting frayed edges will also be different colours.*

Getting it right

If a fabric frays very easily, it can be best to stitch it to the card before you fray the edges. Fray a scrap first to assess the best way of using the fabric. Sometimes the warp and weft threads are of a different thickness, so in one direction the frayed edge will be dense and lush and in the other, fine and delicate.

Ideas & inspiration

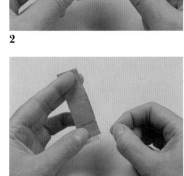

Experiment with fraying different fabrics; pieces cut from an old silk tie make a simple and bold statement (left).

Drawn thread work is a development of this technique – fibres are pulled from the body of the fabric rather than the edge (above). Fabric with white warp and gold weft threads looks pretty and delicate with threads drawn out from both directions to create a lacy plaid effect.

69 Using transparent fabric

Transparent or semi-transparent fabrics, like acetate or plastic (with which they are often interchangeable), are best attached to a card with machine stitching rather than adhesive. Use these fabrics to provide a sheer or subtle background for other applications, or take advantage of the see-through quality and make a pocket to either protect or contain other materials.

1 Cut a square of tulle with pinking shears and stitch it to a card, leaving an opening in the bottom edge. If the fabric frays, make frayed edges (see *68 Fraying fabric*, page 70) or use zigzag stitch.

1

2 Push sequins under the fabric. Stitch the opening closed, overlapping a few stitches at either end through the previous stitching holes.

2

Ideas & inspiration

Organza ribbons are inexpensive, easy to store, widely available and have only two edges that fray. A neat, uniform edge is achieved with zigzag stitch and transparent thread (right).

Stitch ribbon over sequins; a nice effect occurs where the sequins overlap (below).

△ *This card uses the same principle as the one made in 65 Stitching acetate and plastic (see page 67), but the tulle gives a softer, more feminine look to the finished card.*

---

70 Simple weaving

Ribbons and strips of fabric can be woven to create entirely new and unique fabrics, though it can be quite a time-consuming process. However, a simpler form of weaving involves threading ribbons or strips of material in and out of an open-weave fabric, such as net. It's a good way to create a woven effect and is very quick if you use ribbon.

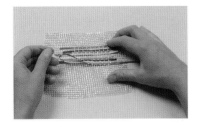

Cut a piece of net larger than the size of the aperture you are going to frame it in. Thread a tapestry needle with each length of ribbon in turn and weave them in and out of alternate holes across the net.

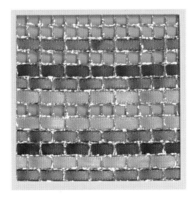

Getting it right
Mount the woven fabric in an aperture card to hide the untidy edges (see *6 Cutting square apertures*, page 18, and *7 Cutting shaped apertures*, page 20).

▷ *Ribbons the same width as the holes in the net are used here, but you could gain more texture by using wider ones that will bunch up when woven.*

Ideas & inspiration

A different interpretation of simple weaving using recycled fabrics. An old cotton chair back has been woven with narrow strips of cotton cut from worn-out shirts (top).

Use the conventional weaving technique to weave your own cloth of many colours from frayed, random-width strips of your favourite fabrics combined with vibrant ribbons (below).

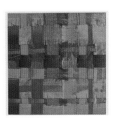

71 Attaching panels with ribbon

This technique provides an elegant way of attaching a panel to a card. The decoration could be applied solely to the paper you are attaching, leaving the card plain. This is ideal where text is needed – on invitations, for example. The words can be reproduced on a photocopier or computer printer, cut to size and attached to the card.

1 Using a ruler and pencil, mark two points at the centre top of the panel, here they are 10mm (½in) down from the top edge and 15mm (¾in) apart. These points indicate the top of the slit that will be cut to accommodate the ribbon. Place the card on a cutting mat and position the panel on the card. Cut a slit through all the layers, working down from the marked points. These slits are 10mm (½in) long.

2 Thread a large-eyed needle with a length of organza ribbon. Carefully pick the card up, making sure the panel doesn't move, and push the needle through the slit on the right, from front to back.

3 Bring the ribbon to the front by passing the needle through the left-hand slit. Pull a generous amount of ribbon through.

4 Repeat the process to tie the panel to the card. Pass the needle through the right-hand slit again, to the back of the card.

5 Bring the ribbon to the front through the left-hand slit. Pull the ribbon through until it lies quite tightly around the slits, securely attaching the panel to the card.

6 Arrange the ends of the ribbon so that they look attractive and balanced. Trim them so that they slant in the same direction.

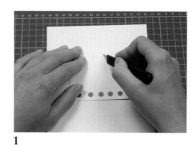

1

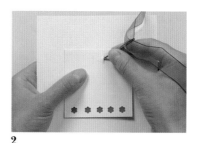

2

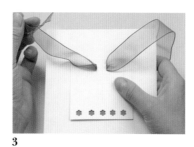

3

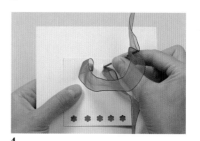

4

△ *This panel is made of two squares of paper, one with a row of punched flower motifs and the second in a contrasting colour. The coloured square is placed behind the punched one and the two are glued together along the top edge to hold them together while you attach them to the card. Organza ribbon, which squashes down to nothing for threading through the card, but springs back out into full tails, adds glamour to the card.*

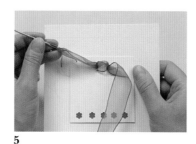

5

6

Getting it right

It will be necessary to use your judgement when deciding on the position, spacing and length of the slits, according to the ribbon or braid you are using. However, the slits must never be longer than the ribbon is wide. If the ribbon compresses, like organza, you will be able to feed it through quite a small slit. If you are using thick or narrow braid, it may be better to punch a small hole to pass it through.

Ideas & inspiration

Use the same technique with narrow braid or matt ribbon for a smart, sophisticated look.

72 Tying perfect bows

Tying a perfect bow is something many of us think we can do, until we try! Bows have all kinds of decorative applications, but one can provide the centrepiece for a card, especially if an object is suspended from it (see 62 Using shells, page 65). This method of tying a bow produces a good result, but needs some practice.

1 To tie a bow directly onto the front of a card, mark and cut two slits to pass the ribbon through. Make the slits as small as you can, while still accommodating the ribbon comfortably.

2 Pass a length of organza ribbon in and out of the two slits. Use a large-eyed needle if you can't push it through with a fingernail.

3 Tie a single knot by passing the tail of ribbon in your left hand over and under the tail in your right hand.

4 Taking the tail on the left, form a loop that points to the top right.

5 Take the tail on the right and bring it up and over the loop, then push it to the right through the new loop just formed to tie the bow.

6 Manipulate the bow, making the loops even and balanced.

7 Decide on the length of the tails. Fold the ends in half widthways and cut them on a slant to make a V-shape in each end.

▷ *Organza ribbon makes particularly good bows, as it can be passed through small holes, is not bulky and produces a full and glamorous final result.*

1

2

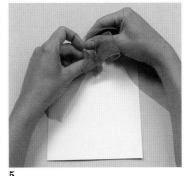
3

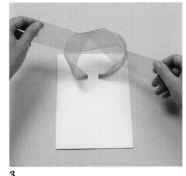
4

5

6

Ideas & inspiration

You can cut slanted ends if you prefer, so that they mirror each other, as shown here. This looks particularly good on contemporary cards, while the V-shaped ends are more traditional.

7

73 Making and using cord

A cord can provide a finishing touch to a card, whether it is functional, decorative, or both. Making a cord is straightforward, though you will need the help of a friend. The twisting means that the cord will be about ten per cent shorter than the threads you started with, depending on how tightly you twist them.

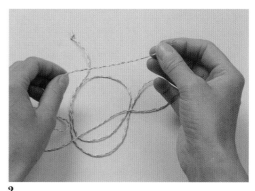

1 Cut lengths of at least three threads and knot them together at one end. Ask a friend to hold firmly on to the knot. Divide the threads into two groups (it doesn't matter if the groups have different numbers of threads in them), and take one group in each hand. Use your fingertips to twist each group clockwise or anti-clockwise; it doesn't matter as long as you twist both in the same direction. It won't work if you twist them in opposite directions.

2 Twist the entire length of the threads, then bring the ends together and ask your helper to let go of the knot. The threads will twist together and make a cord.

3 Tie the cord around the fold of the card with a double knot.

4 Thread a button onto either end of the cord. Keep the button in place with a knot, then trim and fray the ends of the cord below the knot to make a small tassel.

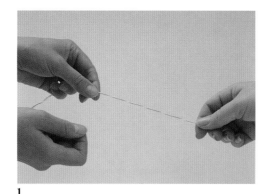

1

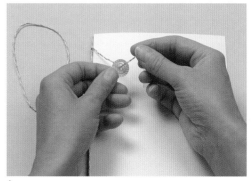

2

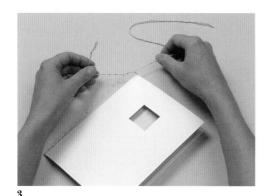

3

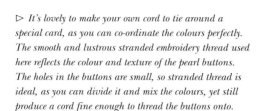

4

▷ *It's lovely to make your own cord to tie around a special card, as you can co-ordinate the colours perfectly. The smooth and lustrous stranded embroidery thread used here reflects the colour and texture of the pearl buttons. The holes in the buttons are small, so stranded thread is ideal, as you can divide it and mix the colours, yet still produce a cord fine enough to thread the buttons onto.*

Ideas & inspiration

The ends of the cord also provide an opportunity to embellish a card further, with such things as (left to right), antique tassels, pom-poms, gilded and drilled wooden shapes, beads, tiny metal bells and drilled shells. Tie or thread them onto the ends of the cord.

Getting it right

Cords are useful if you want to make a lot of invitations, for a party, for example. Buy card blanks and ribbon or cord to tie around the fold and hold an internal sheet in place. Have sheets of paper printed with the invitation details and fold them to make internal sheets (see *8 Internal sheets*, page 21). Then slip the sheets into the cards and tie the cords around the fold.

Punching and piercing

Punching, piercing and perforating paper or card must be among the simplest and most straightforward of all forms of surface decoration. Worked directly onto the card surface, or on a panel that is mounted onto the card, the results can look elegant and understated. Colour need not be involved in these cards, they will make use of light and shade to create subtle and very lovely effects. Also included in this chapter is piercing metal foil. Foil is very thin and can easily be pierced, or punched, using any of the techniques illustrated. Be careful when working with metal foil, as the edges can be sharp.

74 Punching

A hole punch used to make two holes in paper for filing can be used to create simple but effective cards. Single hole-punches are also available and either of these can replace the leather punch used here. However, a leather punch is useful for lots of applications, as it can make holes of different sizes and is also strong enough to make holes in thick card.

1

1 Cut a panel of thin card and punch a row of evenly spaced holes along one edge.

2

2 On the wrong side, apply a thin line of adhesive either side of the row of holes. A glue-stick is ideal for this (see *21 Paper adhesive*, page 31).

3

3 Stick a piece of kitchen foil to the adhesive, covering the holes.

4

4 Use the glue-stick to apply adhesive all over the back of the panel.

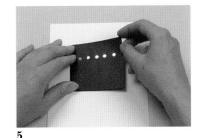

5

5 Position the panel carefully and press it onto a card.

◁ *Most punches have a limited reach, so you can't punch a hole in the middle of a card. Get round this by punching a piece of paper to be applied to a card. Alternatively, range the holes down the leading edge of the card and emphasize them with a coloured internal sheet (see 8 Internal sheets, page 21).*

Ideas & inspiration

Use a leather punch to punch a row of holes decreasing in size. If they are punched in thick card, then the element of shadow is also introduced (top).

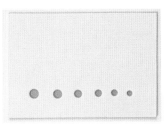

Punch an uneven row of holes in a strip of coloured card with a slot-shaped punch (below). Tie the strip onto the card with narrow ribbon (see *71 Attaching panels with ribbon*, page 72). Use the slot punch to make the holes for the ribbon in the coloured strip, but a craft knife to cut the aligning slots in the front of the card.

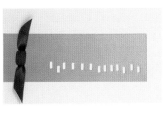

75 Punching shapes

Shaped paper punches can be bought in most craft and hobby stores and are available in a wide range of designs. Though they produce simple shapes, they can be the foundation of original, creative and quick cards.

1 Punch holes in a pattern in two colours of thin card.

2 Arrange the punched paper on a card and stick it in place with paper adhesive (see *21 Paper adhesive*, page 31). Stick down the punched-out pieces of card, too, to make a pattern of positive and negative shapes.

1

2

△ *It is better to use thin card rather than paper, as the card gives the design a slight relief and makes it more interesting.*

Ideas & inspiration

Relief mount (see *98 Relief mounting*, page 97) a strip of punched card so that the punched shapes create shadows on the card, adding interest to a simple design.

Getting it right

Save the punched shapes, even if they are of no use at the time. Use them as confetti in an envelope or trap them behind acetate (see *65 Stitching acetate and plastic*, page 67) or fabric (see *69 Using transparent fabric*, page 71).

76 Piercing paper

This technique covers three ways of piercing paper. Dressmaker's tracing wheels have either sharp, needle-points or blunt teeth. The sharp type pierces holes and the toothed variety makes indentations. A needle allows you to create complex motifs, though this does take some time. A sewing machine with no thread produces evenly spaced pierced holes quickly.

Using a tracing wheel

1 Open the card out flat and place it on a cutting mat. Roll a blunt-toothed tracing wheel across the surface of the card in wavy lines. Applying different pressures as you roll along, and the surface you place the card down on, can produce different lines or deeper indentations, so experiment on some scrap paper before you start a project.

2 A slightly softer surface, such as corrugated cardboard, or a kitchen sponge, is better if you want to use a needle-point wheel to pierce the paper.

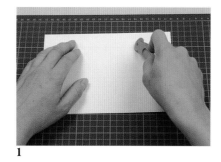

1

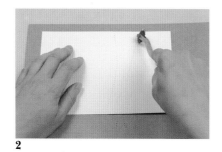

2

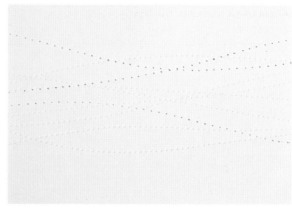

△ *Both types of tracing wheel leave perfectly spaced, even-sized marks in their wake. Here they have been used to make multiple lines across the front of a card for a minimal and contemporary look. And it takes about a minute to make!*

Using a hand-sewing needle

1 Transfer a motif onto the card (see *40 Transferring a template*, page 43).

2 Use a fine sewing needle to pierce small holes in the more intricate parts of the design, in this case the curly parts of the lines. It is important to space the holes as evenly as possible for the best effect. Move on to a thicker needle and pierce larger holes along the main sections of the design. When you have pierced the whole design, rub out the pencil lines with a soft eraser.

1

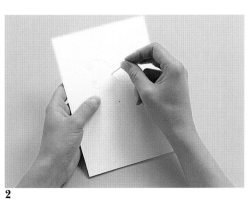

2

◁ *The subtle effect of piercing can make even the simplest design effective.*

Ideas & inspiration

Make more of a pierced design by making holes from both sides of the card. This will give a combination of flat holes and raised holes – a delicate relief on the smooth surface of the card.

Using a sewing machine

1 For this technique it's better not to transfer an image directly onto the surface of a card, as it may be difficult to rub out the pencil lines afterwards. Copy a design onto tracing paper, then position it on the card and hold it in place with masking tape.

2 Test the stitch on some scrap paper and set the stitch length. Do not use a very close stitch or you will cut out the shape rather than pierce it. Stitch around the design, being careful not to over-run at the corners, and turn the corners with the needle down through the card to make nice sharp right angles.

3 Carefully peel off the tape and remove the tracing paper to reveal the pierced design.

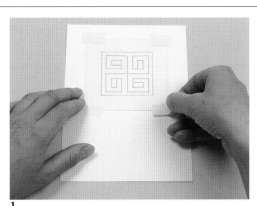

1

2

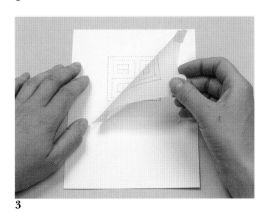

3

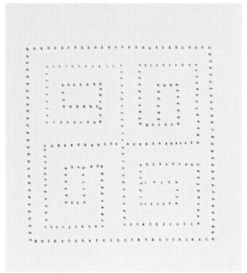

▷ *The designs produced using this method can be as simple or as complex as you want. You can also use a fancy embroidery stitch (see 15 Perforating edges, page 26).*

77 Piercing metal foil

Thin metal foil is a wonderful material for card makers – it's easy to work with, lends itself to many decorative techniques and gives the simplest designs an ornate touch. Here piercing by hand is combined with simple embossing.

1 Photocopy a design, cut it out and stick it to a piece of copper foil with low-tack spray adhesive.

2 Using a dried-up ballpoint pen, lightly draw over all the lines of the design to transfer them onto the foil.

3 Peel off the paper template. Decide which parts of the design you want to pierce and which parts you want to emboss. With the ballpoint pen, and working on the back of the design, draw firmly over the lines that you want to emboss.

4 Clamp a needle into a needle vice and pierce holes along the lightly drawn lines with the needle. Take care to space the holes as evenly as possible.

5 Cut out the design with a pair of sharp scissors. Do not use your best scissors, as the foil will blunt them. Using all-purpose adhesive (see *22 All-purpose adhesive*, page 31), stick the foil design to the front of the card.

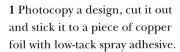

Getting it right

You can tint the foil by rubbing the surface with antiquing wax, which is available in a wide range of colours.

1

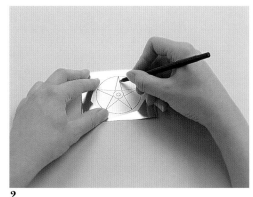

2

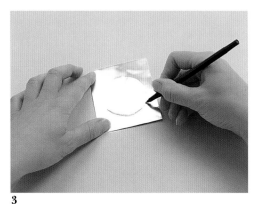

3

4

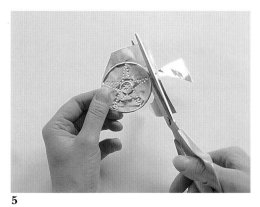

5

△ *Emboss the design from the back and pierce it from the front to create the strongest contrast. To frame the design on a card, stick a square of coloured or textured paper to the front of the card, then stick the copper foil to the square.*

78 Perforating

Related to piercing, perforating uses a line of pierced holes made with a sewing machine with no thread to guide the direction of a tear. It's a fun way to introduce a subtle three-dimensional element that relies on the play of light and shadow to create impact. Edges can be decorated in this way, too (see 15 Perforating edges, page 26).

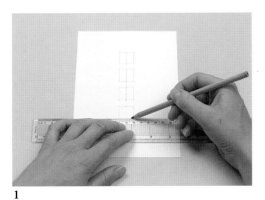

1

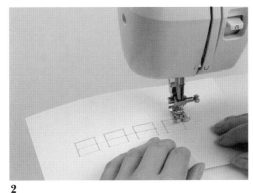

2

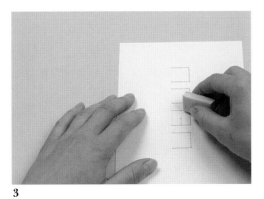

3

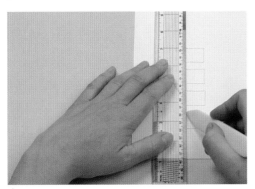

4

5

◁ A row of 'windows' open to reveal some holographic paper, although anything from a photograph to a pressed flower could be hidden behind them.

1 Using a pencil and ruler, measure and lightly mark out four squares down the centre of a card.

2 Set a sewing machine to a fairly close straight stitch and stitch around three sides of each square, leaving the left-hand side unstitched.

3 Rub out pencil marks with a soft eraser.

4 Position a ruler against the left edges of the squares, ensuring that it is parallel to the edge of the card. Use a bone folder to score a short line down the un-perforated left-hand edge of each square, joining the top and bottom perforated lines

5 Gently and carefully push the windows open along the perforated lines. Stick a piece of holographic paper behind the windows (see *21 Paper adhesive, page 31*).

Getting it right
Always test the stitch first. The stitch length must not be too long, or the holes will be too far apart to be easily torn. If it is too short the needle will cut along the line as you stitch and you won't get a perforated effect.

Ideas & inspiration
Emphasize the effects of light and shade in an abstract card (right), by relief mounting the perforated panel (see *98 Relief mounting, page 97*).

There are three other possible ways of using perforations (below). First, the perforations can be made, but the paper left in place, as in the centre squares. Second, the perforated shapes can be removed, as with the right-hand squares. Lastly, the squares removed can be stuck back on as surface decoration and to provide depth, as on the left.

Using botanicals

Botanicals – used here as a generic term to describe anything of plant-based origin – offer great scope for decorative card making. They are abundant, unique and beautiful, and many of them are free! Flowers are the queens of botanicals – delicate, fragile, colourful, luxurious and romantic – and leaves are the kings. When designing a card with botanicals, consider the composition carefully and give the material importance with repeated use or careful placing. Please respect the countryside when you are collecting botanicals; don't take rare flowers or damage plants and trees.

79 Preparing botanicals

There are three main types of botanical – flowers, leaves, and seeds and particles – and each type needs a different method of preparation. Described here are the methods that are generally most effective.

Preparing flowers

Flowers can be preserved in a number of ways, but pressed flowers are the most practical type for decorating cards. Some flowers press better than others and it really is a question of trial and error. Thick-petaled or fleshy flowers won't work at all and other flowers lose their colour, or simply fall apart in the pressing process. There are many specialist books on pressing flowers you can refer to, but trying out a flower yourself is part of the fun.

A simple wooden flower press is inexpensive and can yield a year-round supply of beautiful embellishments for cards. The important thing to remember is that flowers should be put into the press in prime condition. There is no point in using flowers past their best, which have been gathered on a wet evening, out of season.

Ideally, collect flowers on a fine, dry day, when the dew has disappeared, and transfer them into the flower press as soon as possible. Keep a flower press in your car for when you are away from home, just in case!

◁ *Daisies, pansies and feverfew press well. Press the individual flowers from composite blooms such as hydrangea and verbena, and individual petals of flowers such as roses and gerberas.*

1 Undo the flower press and lift off the layers of card and paper to reveal the lower of two sheets of blotting paper. Place the items on the paper, ensuring that they don't touch. If you want to press flower stems, it's best to remove them from the flower head and press them separately. They can be stuck back into position on the card.

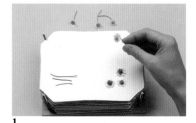

2 Place a second piece of blotting paper over the top of the material, followed by a layer of corrugated cardboard.

3 Close the press, screwing it up tightly. Tighten the screws a little more now and again, when you remember. Most items are dry within a week, depending on thickness and humidity.

Getting it right

The paper supplied in some flower presses is not always as good as it could be, so it's often worth replacing it with thick, good quality blotting paper, as the better absorbency helps the flowers to dry more quickly. It's also important to try and keep the flowers a consistent thickness across each layer, or thick ones will prevent thin ones from being gripped snugly between the layers. Different thicknesses in different layers are better.

Preparing leaves

You can sometimes buy preserved leaves and prepared skeleton leaves are widely available. Both can be applied to the surface of a card without further preparation.

However, the trees and plants in your garden can provide a wealth of different leaves. Use fresh ones and prepare them by drying them in a flower press (see *Preparing flowers*, page 80), which keeps them flat and makes the most of their beautiful shapes and forms.

Many leaves press well, retaining their colour. Walk around a park looking for likely candidates and be waiting there in autumn as they drop their bounty!

▷ *Some of the bigger, oval leaves will look dull, so look out for smaller, interestingly shaped and coloured leaves, such as ivy, hawthorn, acer, and fern leaves.*

Preparing seeds and particles

Almost all supermarkets will have an array of seeds to choose from that require no further preparation. Items such as fennel, sunflower and pumpkin seeds can be used straight from the jar or packet in which they were bought.

Particles are tiny sections of plants, such as the individual heads of a lavender stem. These can be bought ready-dried from florists and craft stores, or you can dry your own by spreading them out on a cloth-covered tray and putting them in a warm place for a few days.

▷ *Asian supermarkets in particular are a great hunting ground for all manner of fascinating and exotic materials, such as red medlar berries, yellow beans and sliced betel nuts.*

80 Attaching flowers and petals

It's important to use the right adhesive for flowers, as some kinds quickly stain or discolour.
A gel formula all-purpose adhesive (see 22 All-purpose adhesive, page 31) gives excellent
results, but use it sparingly. With larger flowers, such as pansies, use a light coating of
spray adhesive (see 29 Spray adhesive, page 35) to stick the entire surface to a card.

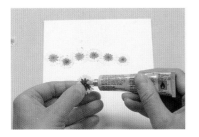

Dab a spot of all-purpose gel adhesive onto the back of the centre of a flower head and gently press it into position on a card.

△ *Create a lasting memory of summer with simple daisies stuck in an uneven row across the front of a card.*

Ideas & inspiration

Poles apart from the faded, dusty arrangements you sometimes find in card stores, a single daisy and four gerbera petals make a modern statement. If you feel that the flowers need further protection, trap them behind acetate (see *65 Stitching acetate and plastic*, page 67).

81 Attaching leaves

Shapely and textural, leaves are a great source of decoration. Skeleton
leaves are best stuck down with spray adhesive (see 29 Spray adhesive, page
35). For pressed and preserved leaves, use the same gel formula all-purpose
adhesive as for flowers (see 80 Attaching flowers and petals, above).

1 Protect the work surface and spray the back of a skeleton leaf with adhesive. Position the leaf over a card, then press it onto the surface. Press with the palm of your hand to ensure that all of the leaf sticks to the card.

2 Apply a little all-purpose gel adhesive to the back of a pressed or preserved leaf and stick it to the card.

▷ *Try gluing the face of the leaf to the card, keeping the underside uppermost, so that the bold veins add further interest. Use your finger to rub a little gold or silver wax over the veins to highlight them further.*

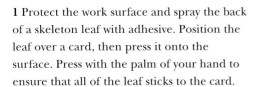

1

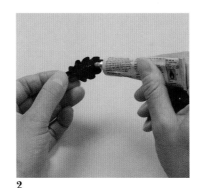

2

Ideas & inspiration

There is a nice correlation between leaves and hand-made paper; maximize this with carefully combined colours and textures.

82 Attaching seeds and particles

Seeds and particles, such as fennel seeds and lavender heads, can add the dimension of scent to a card. Double-sided film (see 27 Double-sided film, page 34) is an effective and clean medium for sticking them down, though many types of seed can also be used successfully behind transparent material (see 69 Using transparent fabric, page 71).

1 Cut three thin strips of double-sided film, each approximately 3–4mm (⅛in) wide. Remove the backing paper, and stick each strip across the front of the card, ensuring that they are straight and equidistant from each other. Here the third of the three strips is being worked on.

2 Trim off any edges that overlap the sides of the card.

3 Peel off a short section of the protective paper. As you work across the film, peel off more of the paper. Exposing only a short section at a time helps to stop the lavender heads falling onto it and sticking in the wrong place.

4 Use tweezers to place each lavender head in position on the tape, keeping them as straight and level as possible. Butt them closely together and place them all the same way up to get a consistent graduation of colour from the top to the bottom of each strip of lavender.

5 Finish by adding a 7mm- (½in-) wide strip of co-ordinating paper just underneath the bottom strip. Use a glue-stick (see *21 Paper adhesive*, page 31) to apply adhesive to the wrong side of the paper, then gently ease it up under the lower edge of the lavender heads and press it down onto the card.

1

2

3

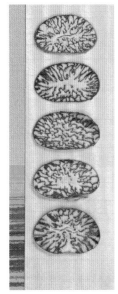
4

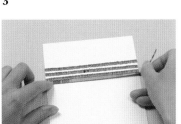
5

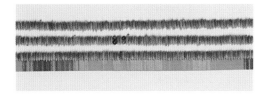

△ *A few tiny beads stuck to the film in between the lavender heads on the middle strip add subtly different colour and texture.*

Ideas & inspiration

Use all-purpose gel adhesive (see *80 Attaching flowers and petals*, page 82) to attach larger seeds. Pumpkin and sunflower seeds can be arranged formally between contrast-coloured papers (below). Leave to dry completely before handling the card.

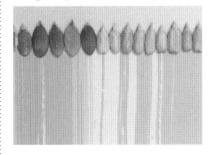

The beautiful markings of sliced betel nuts are shown off perfectly when they are stuck to a piece of wood veneer (left).

Collage

Collage is a combination of art and craft which involves bringing together different materials that are arranged and layered to create new surfaces, patterns, textures and images. The versatility of the medium stems from the huge variety of materials that can be incorporated, making collage a very personal means of expression. As we are dealing with collage for card making, paper forms the basis for the following techniques and the results are two-dimensional. However, you could extend the ideas and create depth and texture using fabrics and found objects in addition to paper.

83 Choosing materials

A huge variety of collage materials can be found at home. Packaging, paper bags, gift wrap, wallpaper, sweet wrappers and magazines are all useful. Combine them with old letters, sheet music, maps, foreign texts, old books on mathematics or engineering and photographs to create interesting and unique cards.

Gather together a variety of different papers, considering such things as type, weight, appearance and surface texture. Papers should be of similar weights or the surface of the collage will be very uneven. It often helps to focus on a particular theme or colour story to give a collage a sense of order. It's also good to provide a focal point for a collaged card, using such items as photographs, images or botanicals.

84 Creating a background

It can be quite difficult to know where to start a collage when faced with a pile of materials, particularly if you lack confidence in your creative ability. This technique is almost foolproof, and should get you headed in the right direction. To decide which section of the background will work best, use L-crops to assess any number of possibilities before you commit yourself. L-crops are simple to make out of thin card.

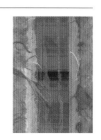

1

1 Tear some selected papers against a steel rule into strips of varying widths (see *13 Tearing against a rule*, page 25).

2

2 Use a piece of sturdy paper to stick the strips to. Generously brush on PVA adhesive in an area slightly longer than the strips. Do not cover the whole surface, it's better to apply the adhesive in stages as you work across.

3

3 Position one strip at a time on the glued background. Brush on more adhesive to completely cover the surface of each strip before applying the next one. Don't worry that the adhesive is white, it becomes clear as it dries.

△ *The stripes create a sense of order and also provide distinct areas that are useful for positioning highlights and embellishments on.*

The strips should overlap each other slightly so that no background paper is visible. Tissue and semi-transparent papers partly laid over stronger patterned papers create some interesting effects. Consider the placing of the various papers and colours, aiming for a balanced and harmonious result. At this point, do not add highlights and embellishments. Leave to dry completely.

4 On a sheet of thin cardboard mark a pair of identical L-shapes. Interlock the Ls at either end to make them as large as possible. The outer edges of the L-crops shown here measure 230mm (9in) and 210mm (8in) and they are 60mm (2½in) wide. Place the card on a cutting mat and use a steel rule and craft knife to cut out the L-crops.

5 Place one L-crop over the other, creating a viewfinder. Hold this over the collaged background and move the L-crops in and out, and up and down, framing different sections of the paper. When you have decided on the best area and shape of background, lay the L-crops down in position. Use a pencil to mark out the area and the steel rule and craft knife to cut it out.

4

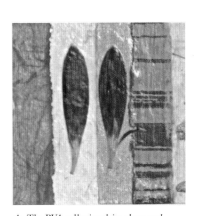
5

85 Laminating

Laminating in this context means bonding materials together using PVA adhesive, which both joins and seals them. This technique works very well on many materials including transparent and semi-transparent papers. Try laminating confetti, sequins, pressed leaves and flowers between layers of tissue paper.

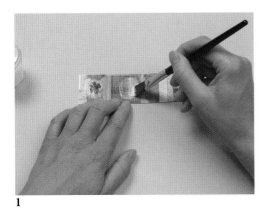
1

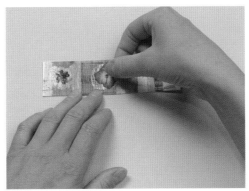
2

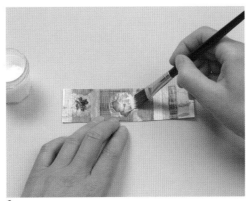
3

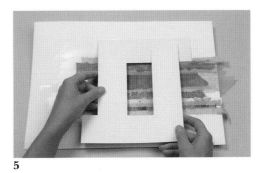
△ *The PVA adhesive dries clear and protects and preserves delicate items like pressed flowers and petals.*

1 Having cut out a background, place some pressed flowers on it and decide on the best arrangement. Remove them and brush a generous amount of PVA adhesive onto the area where each flower will sit. Always apply the adhesive to the card, not the flower.

2 Position the flowers on the glued surface.

3 Very carefully brush more PVA adhesive over each flower to seal it and form a protective covering. Leave to dry completely.

86 Ageing photocopies

If you want to use a photograph in a collage, it's usually better to use a photocopy rather than the original. You can enlarge or reduce the image to suit the card and you can keep the original picture. However, a photocopy can be rather stark. Use tea or coffee to tint the paper a little, or strengthen the liquid further to give the photocopy an aged look.

Mix up a strong solution of coffee powder and cold water. Dip some cotton wool into this and rub it over the photocopy. Repeat the procedure until you achieve the depth of colour you want. Leave to dry completely.

▷ *The sepia tone that coffee gives a photocopy is appropriate for a nostalgic image such as this one. Make a background to complement the image and stick the photocopy to it with spray adhesive (see 29 Spray adhesive, page 35).*

87 Images on acetate

Another way of using an image is to superimpose it on a background. Photocopy the image onto a sheet of clear acetate and when the image is positioned on the collage, the background is visible through the acetate.

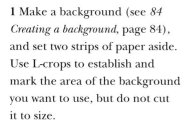

1 Make a background (see *84 Creating a background*, page 84), and set two strips of paper aside. Use L-crops to establish and mark the area of the background you want to use, but do not cut it to size.

2 Cut the acetate image to size, leaving a border on the left- and right-hand sides. Position the image on the collage. Apply PVA to the back of one of the strips of paper you set aside and position it on the card, just overlapping the edge of the acetate. Repeat on the other side to hold the acetate to the background. Leave to dry completely. Cut the background to size and mount it on a card.

1

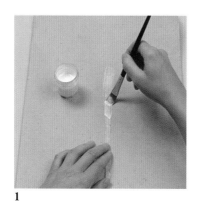
2

△ *Choose papers that are not too brightly coloured or busy for the background, or the image might get visually lost.*

Embossing

Embossing, or the raising of a surface pattern on paper or card, is a commercial production technique that is often used to lend an expensive, up-market look to stationery such as covers, folders and luxury packaging. The design is created by pressing the paper between positive and negative metal plates. There are several simple ways that you can create an embossed effect at home without the need for such plates. A stencil or embossing powder can be used directly on a card. However, if you want to emboss designs in a flower press, emboss them onto panels of paper and mount these onto a card.

88 Embossing with a stencil

This technique creates an effect close to commercially produced embossing. It involves using a tool to force the paper into a stencil and so transfer the image onto the paper. For complex and intricate results you can buy special pierced-metal stencils, of which there are lots available, but it's easy to make your own stencil for simple shapes.

1

2

3

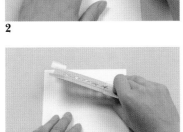

4

◁ *Avoid rubbing over the edge of the stencil, or its outline will also appear on the front of the card.*

1 Transfer a design onto a piece of medium-weight card (see *40 Transferring a template*, page 43). Place the card on a cutting mat and cut out the motifs with a craft knife (see *44 Stencilling*, page 47). Thick card will be too difficult to cut, so recycle cardboard food packaging, such as cereal boxes, wherever you can; they are ideal for making stencils.

2 Because the paper has to be pushed into the stencil, you need to use an uncoated paper with long or random fibres (see *1 Choosing card and paper*, page 14) to be sure

that the paper won't split. Test the paper out before you start. Tape the stencil in position on the right side of the card with masking tape.

3 Working on the wrong side of the card, gently use an embossing tool or a dried-up ballpoint pen to push the paper into the cut-out motifs. Make sure that the tool you use isn't too fine, or you may push through the paper.

4 Carefully peel off the masking tape, remove the stencil and turn the card over to reveal a raised impression of the original design.

Ideas & inspiration

Speed the process up considerably with the help of a shaped paper punch. Here a star-shaped punch was used to make a quick and easy stencil.

Getting it right

The embossing process requires you to work from the back of the card, so that the paper is pushed into the stencil from behind. Unless you are lucky enough to own a light-box, place the card face-forward against a window, so that you can see the position of the motifs through the paper. Using the embossing tool, lightly rub over the back of the card to outline the shapes. Then place the card face-down on a work surface and complete the process.

89 Embossing in a press

Embossed images can also be created in a flower press. Instead of cutting out stencils (though you can use them with this technique), use any reasonably flat items to create an impression. As with 88 Embossing with a stencil (see page 87), an uncoated, forgiving paper, such as blotting paper or watercolour paper, creates the strongest impressions.

1 Cut a piece of blotting paper large enough to accommodate two star-shaped sequins. Wet your hand and pat some water onto the surface of the paper. Don't soak it, but make sure that the area where the sequins will sit is dampened.

2 Open a flower press and put in a piece of smooth card to prevent the corrugated cardboard in the press making any impression. Ideally, use a piece of card cut from food packaging, such as a cereal box, placed printed side up. This card is usually coated to give it a smooth and shiny surface that repels moisture and won't stick to damp paper. Cover the smooth card with a sheet of kitchen towel and then place the piece of dampened blotting paper in the centre. Position the sequins carefully on the paper.

1

2

3

4

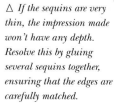

△ *If the sequins are very thin, the impression made won't have any depth. Resolve this by gluing several sequins together, ensuring that the edges are carefully matched.*

3 Lay a sheet of paper kitchen towel over the top, being careful not to move the sequins.

4 Cover the kitchen towel with another piece of smooth card, printed side down this time. Re-assemble the press, screwing it up

tightly. Leave it for about four hours to allow the paper to dry around the sequins. If you remember, try tightening the press up a little more now and again. Undo the press and remove the layers until you reach the sequins and blotting paper. If the paper is dry, remove the sequins to reveal the embossed shapes. If the paper is still damp, lift it out, with the sequins still in place, and lay it on a dry sheet of paper kitchen towel. Allow the paper to dry out completely before removing the sequins.

Ideas & inspiration

Use a key blank to create a classy welcome card for new neighbours (right).

An embossed lucky horseshoe makes a change from traditional wedding cards (far right).

Christmas tree decorations, such as plastic snowflakes, can make a lasting impression (below).

Getting it right

Technically, if the image is raised from the paper, it is embossed; if it is pressed into the surface, it is debossed. The strongest relief will be made on the side the item is pressed against, so the examples shown here are all debossed. In some instances a debossed panel can be difficult to apply to a card, as there is an uneven surface to glue. If so, use an alternative method of attachment, such as an eyelet (see *31 Eyelets*, page 36).

90 Embossing with a pen

This technique is easy and makes both motifs and text look special. Craft shops carry a huge range of embossing materials, but a few basics will get you started. The very fine powder comes in many colours and you can buy an embossing pen that contains a special slow-drying ink, giving you time to write a message, or draw a design, before sprinkling on the powder.

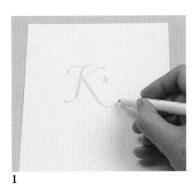

1 Using an embossing pen, draw an initial letter freehand onto a card. Look out for dual-ended pens like this one: one end is a chisel tip that can be used at an angle, rather like a calligraphy pen, and the other end is fine, good for drawing detail.

2 Lay the card on a piece of scrap paper and sprinkle powder all over the design.

3 Shake the excess powder off the card on to the scrap paper, so that it can easily be tipped back into its container.

4 For a perfect finish use a soft paintbrush to carefully remove any specks of powder that may have adhered to the card around the design.

5 Use a dry domestic iron to melt the powder and create the finished effect. Hold the card over the soleplate a little distance away to avoid scorching or distorting the paper. It takes time for the reaction to happen, but it's fun to watch the transformation. Once the powder has melted, do not keep heating it. You can buy a special heat tool for this process, which might be a good investment if you become really keen on embossing, but the embossed cards in this book were all done using an iron.

1

2

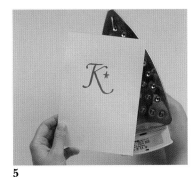

3

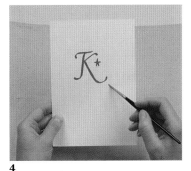

5

△ *Personalize a card for a friend by embossing their initial on the front.*

4

Getting it right

If you are worried about drawing letters freehand, trace them off and transfer them onto a card (see *40 Transferring a template*, page 43). Draw carefully over the pencil with the embossing pen and the powder should end up hiding the pencil marks.

Ideas & inspiration

Give the initial more emphasis and importance by embossing it onto a panel of coloured paper and then relief mounting the panel (see *98 Relief mounting*, page 97).

91 Embossing with a stamp

As an alternative to the freehand method (see 90 Embossing with a pen, page 89), create metallic effects using a rubber stamp with embossing powder. The embossing powder comes in different metallic colours and you can create multi-coloured effects by sprinkling different colours onto the same motif. Store excess mixed powder in a small container for future use.

1 Press a stamp onto an embossing ink pad and then stamp onto a card.

2 Before the ink dries, sprinkle embossing powder over the card, covering all of the stamped design. Tip the excess powder back into the pot to be used again.

3 Use a soft paintbrush to brush off any specks of powder clinging to the card around the stamped motif.

4 Hold the card close to the soleplate of a hot, dry domestic iron until the powder melts and fuses together. Do not let the card touch the iron in case it scorches or distorts it and once the powder has melted, do not keep heating it.

1

2

3

4

△ *Available in lots of lovely designs, rubber stamps can produce intricate images that can be repeated many times over.*

Ideas & inspiration

Emboss white glitter stars onto tracing paper for a frosty card to celebrate the winter holidays. Mount the embossed tracing paper in an aperture (see *6 Cutting square apertures*, page 18), to make the most of its transparency.

Metallic effects

Metallic decoration and embellishment is ever-popular, adding a luxury and opulence to a card that is impossible to emulate with any other materials. Real gold leaf is, not suprisingly, costly, but Dutch metal leaf is inexpensive and is available in imitation gold, aluminium and copper finishes. There are also some lovely novelty finishes, which include variegated colours and all-over motifs. Two types of metal leaf are available – loose leaf and transfer leaf. Both do the same job, but transfer leaf is easier to use. Another versatile metallic product is glitter, familiar to most of us from childhood, and still fun to use.

92 Gilding with a stamp

The usual method of gilding involves the freehand application of gold size (a special adhesive for attaching metal leaf) with a paintbrush, prior to sticking on the leaf. Here a stamp provides a motif for a gilded card, making this a particularly useful technique if you are nervous about painting your own design.

1 Using a paintbrush, brush gold size across the surface of a stamp.

2 Position the stamp carefully over the card, then press it onto the surface to transfer the gold size. Lift off the stamp and leave the size to go tacky according to the instructions on the packaging, usually about 15 minutes.

3 Holding a sheet of gold leaf by the tissue paper it is backed with, carefully lay it over the stamped motif. Smooth over the back of the tissue paper with your fingers to ensure that the leaf sticks to the size, then peel off the paper.

4 Remove the excess leaf from around the motif by carefully brushing it away with a clean, dry soft paintbrush. Store the leaf in a jar for future use.

5 Metal leaf will tarnish in time. Delay this by spraying it lightly with hair lacquer.

1

2

△ *Variegated-colour metal leaf adds an extra decorative element to a simple stamped motif.*

3

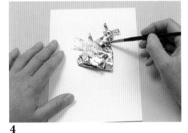
4

5

Getting it right

Metal leaf is extremely thin and light – do not sneeze while you are working! If you find it difficult to handle, try lightly dusting your fingers with talcum powder to absorb any moisture before touching the leaf.

Ideas & inspiration

Gild a sheet of paper, punch out shapes, then mount them onto a card (right). This is a good way to practise handling leaf and the result will be useful for many applications.

Gild some gunmetal paper with a row of stamped silver stars for a subtle metallic effect (below).

93 Gilding with a size pen

If you want to create original designs rather than using a stamp, then using a size pen to apply the gold size is often much easier than applying it with a paintbrush, especially for fine details. You can trace a motif and transfer it to a card if you prefer (see 40 Transferring a template, page 43). Just make sure that pencil marks are covered with size, so that they will be concealed by the metal leaf.

1 Use a size pen to draw a motif directly onto the card. Leave it for about 15 minutes, or the length of time recommended on the packaging, to go tacky.

2 Holding a sheet of metal leaf by the tissue paper it is backed with, carefully lay the leaf over the motif.

3 Smooth over the back of the tissue paper with your fingers to ensure that the leaf sticks to the size, then peel off the paper.

4 Brush off the loose leaf with a soft, dry paintbrush and store it in a jar for future use.

5 Seal the surface of the leaf with hair lacquer to delay any tarnishing.

1

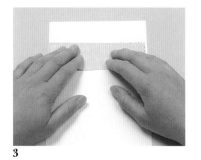
2

3

4

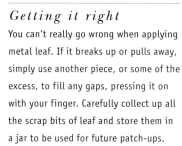

△ *Gild a simple repeated star motif with aluminium leaf. The results have a lovely hand-drawn effect, especially where the edges of the leaf are slightly rubbed away or uneven.*

5

Getting it right
You can't really go wrong when applying metal leaf. If it breaks up or pulls away, simply use another piece, or some of the excess, to fill any gaps, pressing it on with your finger. Carefully collect up all the scrap bits of leaf and store them in a jar to be used for future patch-ups.

Ideas & inspiration
Embellish a gilded motif further for a more intense metallic effect. These gold stars have pearlized star sequins stuck in their centres (below). Use a size pen to create gilded letters or words (right), tracing them out first if you prefer (see *40 Transferring a template*, page 43). This letter has been further embellished with a fine glitter heart on double-sided film (see *27 Double-sided film*, page 34).

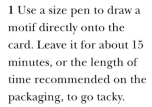

94 Using metallic papers

A selection of the many types of metallic papers available – tissue, wallpaper, holographic gift-wrap, gilded paper and gold and gunmetal cards – are combined to create a simple but effective three-dimensional card. This technique uses sticky mounting pads to attach the stars (see 28 Sticky mounting pads, page 35).

1 Use a small star-shaped paper punch to cut out 16 stars.

2 Measure and mark out a square grid on the card, with a pencil dot to indicate the centre of each of the 16 stars. These stars are spaced 25mm (1in) apart, but the spacing can be adjusted to suit any size of punch or card.

3 Remove the backing paper and stick a small square sticky mounting pad on top of each pencil dot.

4 Peel the remaining protective paper from each sticky pad in turn and apply a star to each one, arranging the colours and textures carefully.

1

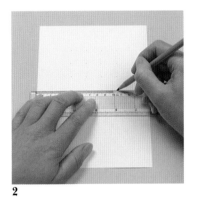

2

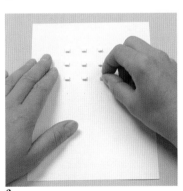

3

4

△ *This is a useful way to use up small scraps of paper, as the technique requires only a tiny amount of each type.*

Ideas & inspiration

Cut a series of 15mm (¾in) squares out of a variety of papers and relief mount them onto a strip of cardboard, which in turn is stuck to a strip of holographic paper. Two sorts of small star sequins add further metallic embellishment (below).

Stick a strip of double-sided film to a card and then stick a mosaic of 15mm (¾in) squares of paper onto that. Enhance the square theme by detailing the mosaic with a row of square sequins (bottom).

95 Using glitter

For high-impact sparkle there's no substitute for glitter. You can buy it in many colours and in various forms. Spraying adhesive (see 29 Spray adhesive, page 35) through a stencil and sprinkling on glitter allows you to create sharp, well-defined metallic motifs.

1   2   3

△ *Glitter for sprinkling varies widely in particle size, from coarse to very fine. The fine type used here is better for keeping the motif edges crisp and straight and provides maximum glitter effect.*

4   5

1 Prepare a stencil (see *44 Stencilling*, page 47) the size of the card, with the motif in the right position. Place the stencil face-down on a protected work surface and spray the back lightly with low-tack spray adhesive.

2 Position the mask on the card and press the two together.

3 Spray an even coat of adhesive over the motif.

4 Remove the mask carefully.

6   7

5 Lay the card on some scrap paper and sprinkle glitter over the motif, ensuring you cover the whole glued area.

6 Tip the excess glitter off the card onto the scrap paper, tapping and shaking the card to remove loose particles. Tip the glitter back into its container.

7 Use a fine paintbrush to brush away stray particles of glitter.

Getting it right
The stencil must cover the surface of the card completely, or glitter will stick to areas it shouldn't! Choose simple, graphic motifs for the best effects.

Ideas & inspiration

Create an alternative metallic effect using double-sided film and accent beads (see *27 Double-sided film*, page 34), which give a lovely texture. Here the star was cut out of a square of film (right).

Add to the decorative effect by applying a glitter motif to printed or decorated paper (far right).

Double-sided film can also be used with glitter. Cut out a motif, peel off the backing paper and position it on a card. Remove the protective paper and sprinkle on the glitter. Shake off the excess to reveal a glittering image (right).

96 Using wire

Wire is available in many types and thicknesses, but thin, brightly coloured craft wire works well with this technique. It is easy to handle and can be used in a number of different ways. In addition to being used to form a shape itself, it can be wrapped around items or objects, or have other items threaded onto it.

1

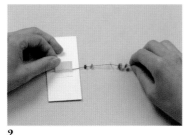

2

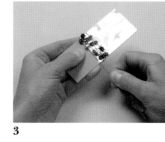

3

4

5

6

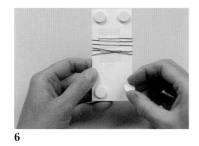

7

1 Thread different-coloured sequins onto coloured wire.

2 Decorate a piece of thick card, as you wish and cut it to an appropriate size. Stick the end of the wire to the back of the piece of card with masking tape.

3 Wind the wire around the card, spacing the sequins out across the front as you go.

4 When you have wound the wire around a few times, cut it off at the back of the card with scissors – not your best ones.

5 Stick the free end of the wire to the back of the card with more masking tape.

6 The winding technique means you will be unable to mount the panel flat onto the surface of the card. Resolve this problem, and take the three-dimensional quality a step further, by attaching the panel to the card with sticky mounting pads (see *28 Sticky mounting pads*, page 35). Stick one to each corner and peel off the protective paper.

7 Position the decorated panel over the card and press it down.

△ *Here the decorated wire is displayed wrapped around a piece of part-gilded card. The colours of the sequins complement the colours in the variegated metal leaf.*

Ideas & inspiration

Make a star shape from soft, pliable wire and suspend it from the centre top of an aperture. The aperture is backed with semi-transparent paper, which allows light to show through and silhouette the star (right).

Wrap a purchased wooden star with beaded wire, then attach it to a background with a sticky mounting pad (far right).

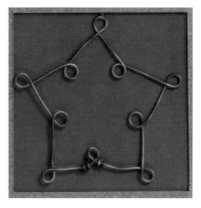

Relief effects

Relief effects, where part or all of the design stands out from the background, can be made out of the surface of the card itself, or can be created on the surface of the card by the application of another material. There will be many occasions when you have prepared pieces of completely flat decoration to apply to a card. Before you stick the decoration straight onto the card, consider using one of the three relief presentation techniques shown here to mount the motif. These methods can enhance the decoration, so make sure you achieve maximum impact and show off your work effectively.

97 Paper-cutting

Creating a motif or pattern by cutting into the surface of the card is a good way to make a relief. Simple motifs are best and some designs may need adapting to retain the small bridges of paper necessary to make the technique work.

1 Transfer a suitable motif onto the front of a card (see *40 Transferring a template*, page 43). Open the card out flat and place it on a cutting mat. Use a craft knife to cut carefully around the pencilled image.

2 Rub out the remaining pencil marks with a soft eraser.

3 Use your finger and thumbnail to carefully lift the cut-out elements up from the surface of the card. Create a gentle crease at the points where they remain attached to the background.

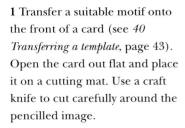
1

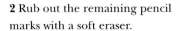
3

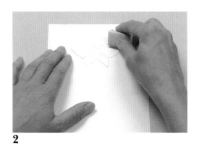
2

Getting it right
The butterfly motif was adapted for this technique by dividing the wings into two sections and transferring only those and the antennae onto the card, omitting the body and head altogether.

△ *The effect is created when elements of the design, still attached to the card by small bridges of paper, are lifted slightly from the surface, allowing the play of light and shadow to enhance the raised shapes.*

Ideas & inspiration

Develop the idea by relief-mounting the paper-cut over coloured paper, which increases the effect of shadow under the wings and creates a coloured line around the edge of the butterfly (left).

Reverse the effect by cutting the butterfly out of iridescent paper and mounting it onto a white card. The whiteness shows beneath the wings, while the iridescence of the cut-out wings creates an interesting effect – sometimes darker and sometimes lighter than the flat background (right).

98 Relief mounting

This is a presentation technique that can create something special out of the mundane and ordinary, or even lift something already quite special to the realms of the extraordinary! It will highlight and draw attention to a decoration or motif, without intruding upon it.

1 Rubber stamp (see *51 Simple stamping*, page 53) a butterfly motif onto a piece of card. Although this doesn't look very interesting as it is, relief mounting it will make a lot of difference.

2 Using a steel rule, tear a square around the motif (see *13 Tearing against a rule*, page 25). Alternatively, cut the edges with a craft knife, shape them with decorative scissors, or perforate them (see *Decorative edges*, pages 25–30).

3 Cut a square of thick card fractionally smaller than the torn panel. Apply strips of double-sided tape (see *26 Double-sided tape*, page 33) along each edge on one side.

4 Peel the protective paper off the tape and stick the thick card to the back of the panel. Position it carefully so that it sits within the torn edges.

5 Apply a strip of double-sided tape to each edge on the back of the piece of thick card. Peel off the protective paper.

6 Position the panel carefully over the face of the card, then press it down.

1

2

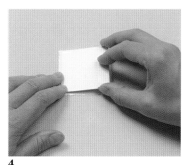

3

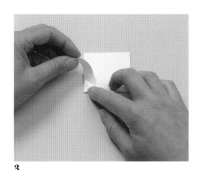

4

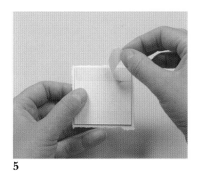

5

6

△ *Relief mounting creates a shadow-line that unobtrusively frames and emphasizes the applied decoration.*

Ideas & inspiration

As an alternative, it is sometimes possible to cut carefully around the edges of a motif before relief mounting it. This works best on compact images with a fairly simple overall shape. If the image is quite large, use a piece of thick card to mount it onto a greetings card. If it is very small, attach it to the card with a sticky mounting pad (see *28 Sticky mounting pads*, page 35).

99 A simple pop-up card

Simple and flexible, this presentation technique allows a motif to be applied in such a way that it rises up from the surface as the card is opened. Any cut-out motif can be attached, whether it is something you have made or a found image.

1 Arrange a cut-out motif on the front of a folded card, in the position you want it to be inside the card. Measure from the folded edge of the card to about 5mm (¼in) over the nearest edge of the motif. Then measure from this point up to the top edge of the card. Note these measurements, as they give the position and the length of the slits you need to cut.

2 Set the motif aside and, using a pencil and ruler, mark the first line you measured on the front of the card. Use a set square to ensure that the line is at right-angles to the folded edge of the card. Mark a second line 10mm (½in) down from and the same length as the first one.

3 Using a steel rule and a craft knife on a cutting mat, cut slits along the two

marked lines. Make sure that you cut through both layers of card.

4 To form a neat crease when you bend the tab inwards, use a bone folder to score a short line joining the inner ends of the two slits. Score on the front and back of the card. Rub out the pencil marks with a soft eraser.

5 Open the card and push the tab through, in the opposite direction to the main body of the card.

6 Use a glue-stick (see *21 Paper adhesive*, page 31) to apply adhesive to the motif where it will be attached to the card.

7 Position the motif on the tab. Allow the adhesive to dry completely before closing the card.

1

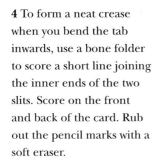
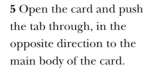

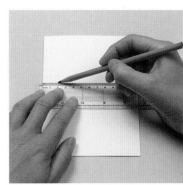

2

3

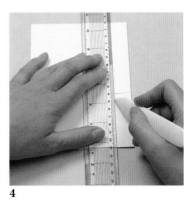

4

5

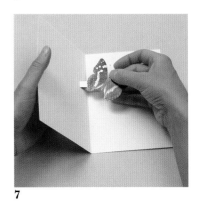

6

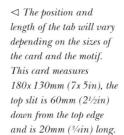

◁ *The position and length of the tab will vary depending on the sizes of the card and the motif. This card measures 180x 130mm (7x 5in), the top slit is 60mm (2½in) down from the top edge and is 20mm (¾in) long.*

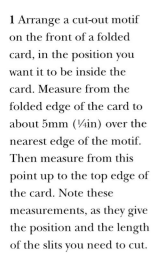

7

100 A simple 3-D card

This is another simple and versatile technique you can use to present your work in a different way. It alters the structure of the card, allowing you to create depth and distance between flat images to achieve a three-dimensional effect.

1 Measure across the front of a folded card and use a pencil to mark the halfway point at the top and bottom.

2 Open the card out flat on a work surface. Use a bone folder to score a line down the front of the card, from top to bottom between the two marked points.

3 Carefully fold the front panel back on itself at the scored line to create a half-size panel. If you have marked and folded accurately, the original open edge of the card front should align with the original folded edge.

4 Position the motif so that it sits halfway across the new fold. To emphasize the three-dimensional effect, position a smaller motif on the back panel of the card.

5 When you are happy with the arrangement, use a glue stick (see *21 Paper adhesive*, page 31) to apply adhesive to the areas of the motifs that will touch the card, then stick them in position. Leave the card open until the adhesive is completely dry.

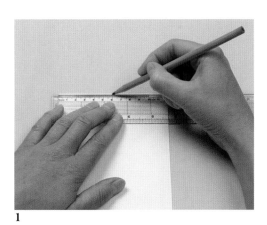

1

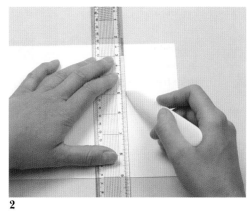

2

3

4

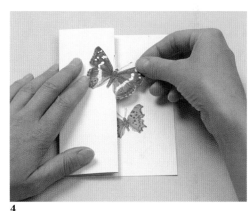

5

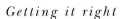

Getting it right

This technique is especially useful if you want to make a card from paper that has different surfaces on each side. When it is folded and standing up, you will see the same surface right across the card.

◁ *If the motif you want to use is not stiff enough to stand out from the edge of the card without drooping, stick it onto a piece of thin card before cutting it out and attaching it to the folded edge.*

Projects

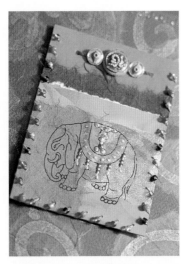

In this section you will find 25 original greetings card projects, ranging from a simple but sophisticated dinner party invitaion, to a nostalgic and romantic card to celebrate a wedding day. All the materials you need to make each card are listed, along with cross-references to all the techniques used, so it's easy to turn back to the relevant technique and study it in detail before trying it out on a card. In addition, all the templates used are given in the Templates section (see page 154).

Making a card need not be a time-consuming job. Shown here are several speedy cards, including the quickest invitation to a child's birthday party you can imagine, and the birthday girl or boy is involved, too. You will also find a wedding invitation and a Christmas card that are easy to produce in large numbers, plus an imaginative card for sending out a photograph in.

However, if you do have the luxury of some time, try one of the more elaborate cards. There are embroidered, beaded, perforated or embossed cards to celebrate birthdays or weddings, or to send to a Valentine – cards that will live up to any occasion.

As well as following the projects shown here, do experiment yourself. Try combining different techniques from the 100 illustrated in the previous section to produce your own unique greetings cards.

Daisy card

Send a cheerful greeting to a friend with a fresh, spring-time card, guaranteed to add a little sunshine to the dullest winter day.

You will need

150 x 300mm (6 x 12in) piece of pale-lime card

Open-weave fabric or lace larger than the card

Low-tack spray adhesive

Brayer

Cream spray paint

Steel rule

Bone folder

70 x 70mm (2¾ x 2¾in) square of lime pearlized card

Pencil

Ruler

Variegated-green stranded embroidery thread

Hand-sewing needle

White beads

Thick card for relief mounting

Double-sided tape

Pressed daisy

All-purpose gel adhesive

Techniques

49 Silhouette spraying, page 51

4 Single-fold cards, page 17

17 Beading edges, page 28

98 Relief mounting, page 97

80 Attaching flowers and petals, page 82

1

1 Do not score or fold the card; this is best done after spraying it, as the sprayed design wraps around to the back. Ensure that the work surface is adequately protected. Spray the wrong side of the fabric or lace with low-tack spray adhesive. The fabric is going to end up covered in paint, so don't use the best tablecloth. Stick the sprayed fabric to the card, checking that the pattern repeat and position looks good. Roll across the surface of the fabric with the brayer to ensure that it is well stuck down. Spray the surface with the cream paint.

2 When the paint is almost dry, carefully peel the fabric off the card. Score and fold it to make a 150 x 150mm (6 x 6in) single-fold card.

3 Mark the position of the stitches along the edges of the square of lime pearlized card and hand-stitch all around with beaded blanket stitch. Thread the beads on so that they sit on the front of the panel. To turn the corners neatly, loop the thread behind the corner of the card.

4 Cut a slightly smaller square of thick card and stick double-sided tape around all edges on both sides. Peel the protective paper off the tape on one side and stick it to the back of the beaded square. Peel the protective paper off the double-sided tape on the other side of the thick card.

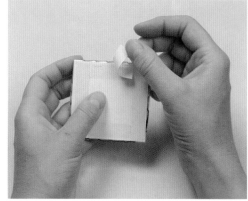

2

3

4

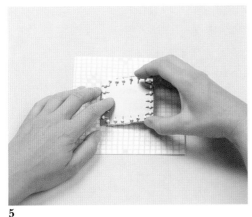

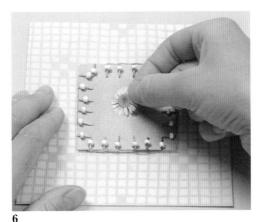

5 Position the decorated square in the centre of the card and press it down firmly.

6 Stick the pressed daisy to the centre of the beaded square with a dab of all-purpose gel adhesive.

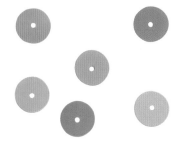

18th birthday

This colourful card traps iridescent sequins in a transparent pocket to make a simple shaker. It looks particularly effective when the light shines through it.

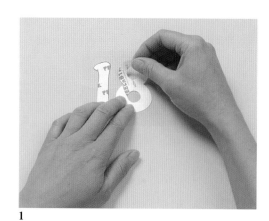

1

2

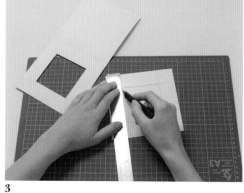

3

4

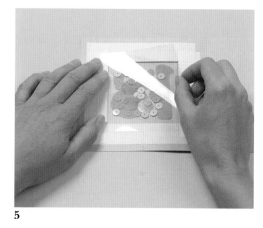

5

1 Enlarge the templates so that they measure 70mm (2¾in) high. Transfer the numbers onto the double-sided film and cut them out with sharp scissors. Peel off the backing paper and stick the numbers to one of the squares of acetate, positioning them centrally.

2 Peel off the protective paper on the front of the numbers and sprinkle on the coloured sand. Shake off the excess onto scrap paper and return it to the container.

3 Prepare the single-fold card by cutting an 80 x 80mm (3in x 3in) square aperture in the front. Cut a corresponding aperture in the square panel of matching card.

4 Place the decorated acetate face-down and centrally in the card aperture. Stick it down all around with masking tape.

5 Place the sequins in the centre of the decorated acetate square. Lay the second square of acetate over the top, trapping the sequins in between. Carefully stick the second square of acetate down all around with masking tape, trapping the sequins in the acetate pocket you have made.

6

7

Getting it right
If you are unsure about where to
position the numbers, cut them out of
plain paper and cut a square of paper
the size of the acetate. Arrange the
numbers on the square and when you
are happy, stick them in place. Lay this
square under a square of acetate and
use it as a template to guide you when
sticking the film numbers.

6 Trim 2mm (⅛in) off the edge of the square
panel that will sit against the inner fold of the
card. Stick double-sided tape around the
edges of the panel and its aperture. Peel off
the protective paper.

7 Position the panel inside the card, ensuring
that the outer edges and the apertures are
perfectly aligned. Press down on the taped
edges to ensure that they are stuck down.

Flower card

A variety of shimmering surfaces make this flower card fresh and fun – a far cry from the staid floral images usually found in card shops. The paper fasteners allow the flowers to rotate.

1 The card is 200mm (8in) high. Score and fold it concertina-style, but with the large panel 150mm (6in) wide and the small ones 50mm (2in) wide. The folded card will fit in a standard-size envelope.

2 Cut three 50mm (2in) high flowerpot shapes out of the sticky-backed plastic, making them approximately 30mm (1¼in) across the top edge and tapering them slightly at the bottom. Use the leather punch to make a row of decorative holes across the top edge of each flowerpot. Peel the backing off the flowerpots and stick them in a row 15mm (¾in) up from the bottom of the folded card, positioning two on the back panel and one on the front-facing short panel.

3 Make holes in the centres of the flower sequins with a leather punch, ensuring that

the holes are large enough to allow the prongs of the paper fasteners to pass through them with ease. Position each sequin in turn directly above its pot, towards the top of the card but at different heights, and make a mark through the centre hole with the pencil. Use the leather punch to make a hole in the card at each pencil mark.

4 To establish the length of the strung sequins required to form the wavy stem of each flower, hold one end just below the hole and cut the string where it touches the top edge of the pot. When you cut the sequins apply a dab of all-purpose adhesive to either end to stop them unravelling. Decide on the position of the pierced leaves by laying each sequin stem in position and using the pencil to mark the top and bottom points of each leaf.

1

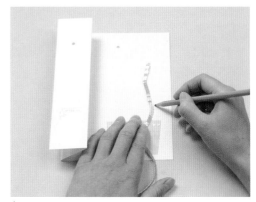
2

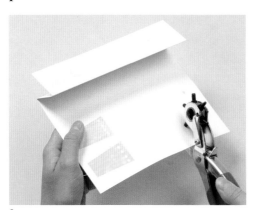
3

4

5

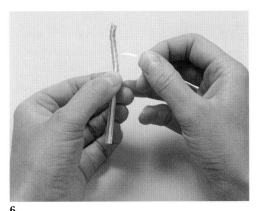

6

7

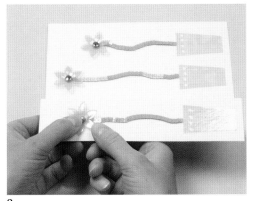

8

5 Pierce the outline of leaf shapes between the pencil marks using a dressmaker's tracing wheel. Rub out the pencil marks with a soft eraser.

6 To stick the sequin stems neatly to the card, use double-sided sticky tape. Cut the tape into very thin strips and stick one to the back of each stem. Peel off the protective paper.

7 Carefully stick the wavy stems in place, from the top of the flowerpot to just below the flower-centre hole. Ensure that the bottom of each pierced leaf touches its stem.

8 Fasten the flowers to the card by passing a paper fastener through the centre of each sequin and through the appropriate hole in the card. Open the prongs out on the back of the card in such a way that the flowers can easily rotate. If you are worried that the points are rather sharp, it's quite easy to square them off using pliers or tin snips before you attach the flowers.

Getting it right

If the flower sequins are pale it may be best to use two for each flower to intensify the colour.

Children's party invitation

Involve a child in pre-party preparations with an easy project to create individual invitations. If the child is particularly keen, the theme could be carried through to decorate paper cups, tablecloths and thank-you notes.

YOU WILL NEED

120 x 120mm (4³⁄₄ x 4³⁄₄ in) orange single-fold card

Multi-coloured ink pad

A willing child

Aprons

Kitchen towels

White ready-mixed poster paint

Paintbrush

Scrap paper

Felt-tip pen

TECHNIQUES

4 Single-fold cards, page 17

Stencilling and printing, pages 47–50

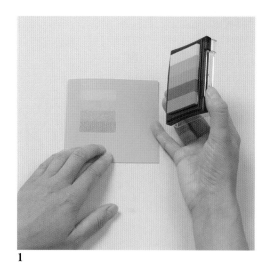

1

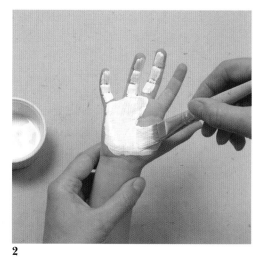

2

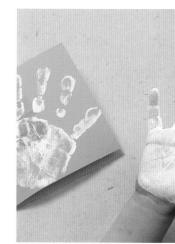

3

4

Getting it right

Often, the second handprint from a single application of paint is better than the first, so observe the results and when printing the invitations, make the first print on scrap paper if necessary.

1 Press the ink pad onto the front of the card to create a coloured rectangle. Print as many cards as is needed, plus a few extra to allow for less successful handprints. Leave the cards to dry completely. Due to the intense pigment in the ink pad this may take a little time, so consider doing it the day before.

2 Protect your clothes and the child's with aprons and keep some kitchen towels nearby to wipe up any accidents. Using a paintbrush, paint the child's hand with white poster paint and help them to practise making handprints on some scrap paper.

3 Print the invitations, re-applying more paint as needed. Help the child to position their hand on the card and press the spread hand down gently with your own to ensure an even print. If you are making lots of invitations, it might be best to wash the child's hand occasionally during the process.

4 Hold the card down while the child lifts their hand off the card surface, then leave it to dry completely. For a final embellishment, the child can write their initial on the card with a colourful felt-tip pen.

Pop-up valentine

This romantic pop-up heart card cannot fail to engage your valentine's attention. If you don't have access to a sewing machine, the heart could just as effectively be made of paper and decorated using other techniques.

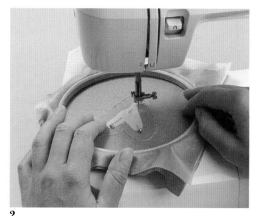
1

2

3

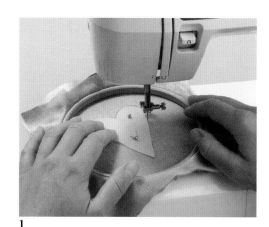
4

1 To make the embroidered heart, apply iron-on interfacing to the back of the pink silk. Lay the crystal organza over the silk and fix the fabrics into an embroidery hoop. Enlarge the large heart template so that it measures 90mm (3½in) long and the small heart template by the same percentage. Trace the hearts onto paper to make two patterns and cut them out. Pin the large heart to the fabric within the hoop and freehand machine stitch around the edge of the pattern with tan thread, going backwards and forwards to create a well-defined line of stitching. Remove the pattern.

2 Pin the smaller heart in the centre of the large one. Stitch the outline in the same way, and then remove the pattern.

3 Fill the gap between the inner and outer heart by stitching continuous spirals all the way around it. Change to silver-grey thread and stitch a chain of small circles around the inside of the inner heart (see main picture).

4 Use sharp scissors to cut around the edge of the heart, close to the stitching. To strengthen the fabric heart and keep it flat, cut a slightly smaller heart out of soft-white card and stick it to the back of the heart.

5

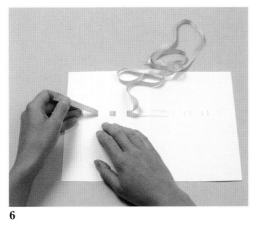

6

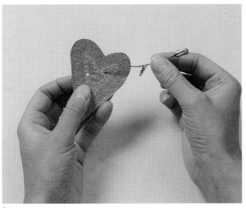

7

8

△ *Tie the ribbons in a perfect bow to close the card, trimming the ends neatly.*

5 On the card cut and score the pop-up tab for the heart. For a heart this size, cut a 30mm- (1¼in-) long slit, 80mm (3in) down from the top. Cut a second slit 10mm (½in) below the first. Cut a series of vertical 10mm (½in) slits, six on each side of the card, in line with the top and bottom of the tab.

6 Open the card out, right-side up, and weave the ribbon through the slits, starting from the middle and passing to the inside of the card through the first slit next to the tab. Thread the ribbon in and out to the left edge, finishing on the front. Apply a little fabric adhesive to the tab and press the ribbon gently onto it. Leave to dry for a few minutes, then repeat the weaving process to the right of the tab, again finishing on the front of the card. Push the tab to the inside of the card.

7 Use the leather punch to make two small holes, angled across the heart, to hold the rosebud. To attach the Cupid, thread it onto the rosebud before you pass the stem in and out of the two holes.

8 Using all-purpose adhesive, stick the heart to the tab. Leave to dry completely before closing the card.

Mono-print card

Mono-printed paper and silk fabric from an old tie, attached with copper rivets, give this card a distinctly masculine feel. Personalize it with rub-down letters and it's undeniably dressed to impress.

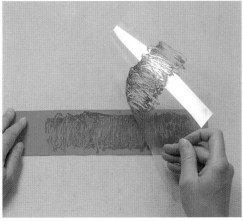

1

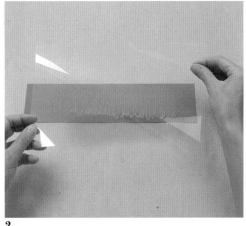

2

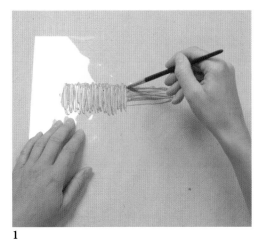

3

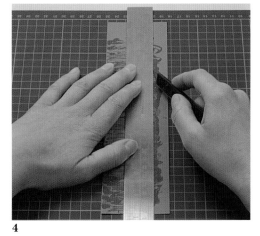

4

5

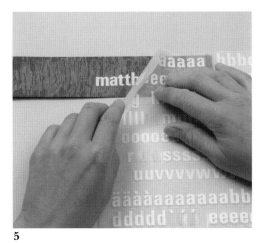

6

7

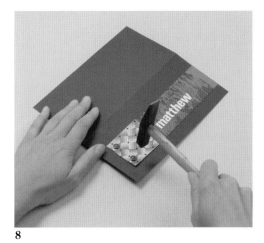

8

1 Squeeze a little orange acrylic paint onto the acetate and use the rubber-tipped paintbrush to scribble through it to make a band approximately 70mm (2¾in) deep.

2 Position the acetate over the ginger paper, paint-side down, then lay it in place. Smooth over the acetate with your hand to transfer the colour and make the print. Carefully remove the acetate and clean off the remaining paint. Leave to dry.

3 Repeat the process with the claret paint. Leave to dry.

4 Place the decorated paper on a cutting mat and use the craft knife and steel rule to cut it into a panel 50mm (2in) deep.

5 Rule a faint pencil line 15mm (⅜in) up from the bottom of the panel. Rub down the appropriate letters. Carefully rub out the pencil line with a soft eraser. Trim the strip to 190mm (7½in) long, with the name approximately 70mm (2¾in) from the left-hand end.

6 Apply iron-on interfacing to the back of the silk, then trim it with scissors so that it measures 53 x 50mm (2¼ x 2in).

7 Use double-sided tape to stick the mono-printed panel to the card, 20mm (⅞in) up from the bottom edge and with the right-hand edges aligned. Lay the rectangle of silk over the left-hand end of the panel, so that the top, bottom and left-hand edges are all aligned. Use the leather punch to punch two holes through all the layers, near to the corners of the fabric.

8 Push the rivets through the holes and hammer them home.

New baby

A special card to mark a special event, this design can easily be made in pink for a traditional baby girl greeting. If you want to be organized and make it in advance, then lemon or lilac would be just as pretty, but you could choose to make a modern statement and celebrate the new arrival with lime or purple!

YOU WILL NEED

Pale-blue thin card

Decorative scissors

Mid-blue ink pad

Cosmetic sponge

Leather punch

Kitchen sponge

Hand-sewing needle

Steel rule

Translucent paper

Pencil

Craft knife

200 x 150mm (8 x 6in) soft-white single-fold card

150mm (6in) of 10mm- (½in-) wide gingham ribbon

All-purpose adhesive

Three small buttons

TECHNIQUES

12 Using decorative scissors, page 25

20 Colouring with an ink pad, page 30

74 Punching, page 75

76 Piercing paper, page 76

13 Tearing against a rule, page 25

4 Single-fold cards, page 17

71 Attaching panels with ribbon, page 72

22 All-purpose adhesive, page 31

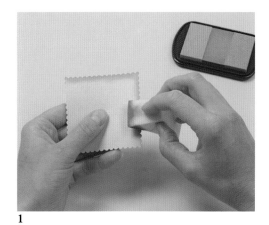

1

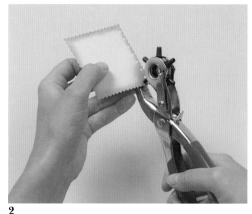

2

3

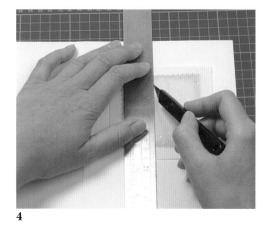

4

1 Use the decorative scissors to cut out a square of blue card measuring 80 x 80mm (3 x 3in). Apply a border of mid-blue around the edges, using the sponge dabbed on the ink pad to transfer a soft haze of colour.

2 Create a pretty border within the darker blue edges, first using the leather punch to make a row of small holes. Space the holes to complement the decorative edge you have cut.

3 Place the square on the kitchen sponge while you embellish the edge further. Use the needle to pierce a diamond of holes in between the punched ones, finishing the corners with four holes pierced in a line.

4 Using the steel rule, tear a square of translucent paper measuring 100 x 100mm (4 x 4in). Open the card blank out flat and position the two squares on the front of the card, with the blue square 40mm (1½in) down from the top edge and the translucent square centred over it. Mark two points, centred on the top edge of the blue square, 10mm (½in) long, 10mm (½in) down from the top edge of the blue square and 15mm (¾in) apart. Use a steel rule and craft knife to cut two vertical slits through all the layers.

5 Feed the ribbon through the slits to attach the two squares to the card. Arrange the ends neatly and trim them.

6 Use all-purpose adhesive to stick three buttons in a row across the translucent paper.

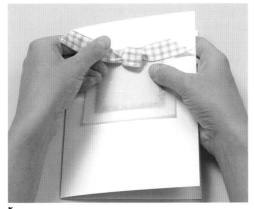

5

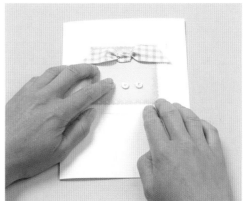

6

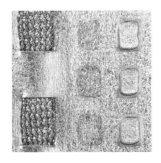

Gilded card

Mix different metallic materials to achieve glowing results. Copper-toned braid, thread and leaf are used here, but you could use gold or silver materials instead.

1

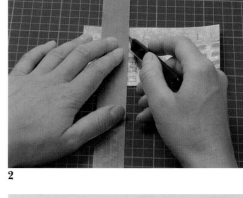

2

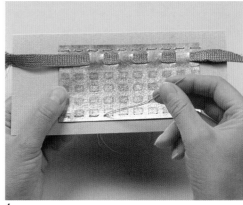

3

4

1 Gild the ochre card by brushing on gold size with the paintbrush rather than a size pen. Apply the copper leaf and the patterned gold leaf next to each other after about 15 minutes. Press the leaf onto the card firmly. Brush away any loose leaf or patch up any missing bits. Seal the metal leaf with hair lacquer to delay tarnishing.

2 Working on a cutting mat, cut the gilded card into a panel measuring 140mm (5½in) high and 75mm (3in) across. Cut the panel so that a 25mm (1in) border of copper leaf runs up the left-edge of the panel – the remaining 50mm (2in) is covered with the patterned gold leaf. Cut eight evenly spaced 10mm- (½in-) wide horizontal slits within the copper border to accommodate the braid.

3 Wrap sticky tape around one end of the metallic braid to prevent it from undoing and to make it easier to thread through the slits. Pass the braid in and out through the slits in the card, beginning and ending on the front of the panel.

4 Stick small pieces of double-sided tape to the centre top and bottom of the panel, remove the protective paper and stick the panel centrally onto the front of the card. The tape will hold the panel in place while you stitch. Thread the needle with the metallic thread and work running stitch up both sides of the panel, making the length of the stitch the same size as the squares on the patterned metal leaf.

5

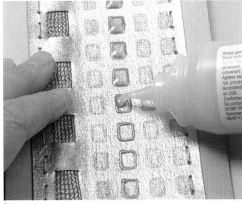

6

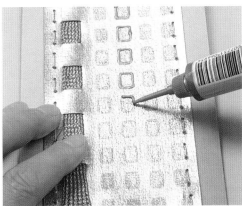

7

5 Trim the ends of the metallic braid and fray them out.

6 Embellish the patterned metal leaf by applying glass-painting outliner around the edges of every square in one column. Leave to dry.

7 Fill in the centre of each of the outlined squares with dimensional liquid. Leave the card to dry completely.

Wedding card

Celebrate a happy union with a card embellished with a pansy, also known as 'heartsease'. This is a time-consuming project, but the results are delicate, lacy and unashamedly romantic.

1 Place the translucent pearlized paper right-side up on a large sheet of scrap paper. Stick a strip of low-tack masking tape down each of the short edges, allowing the ends to overlap and stick to the scrap paper.

2 Spray the wrong side of the lace with low-tack adhesive and lay it over the pearlized paper, ensuring that the pattern is thoughtfully positioned. Roll over the lace

with the brayer to ensure that it is well stuck down. The lace will be covered in paint, so don't use anything too precious.

3 Spray evenly across the surface of the lace with the pale cream paint.

4 Before the paint is completely dry, remove the lace and peel off the masking tape. Leave to dry.

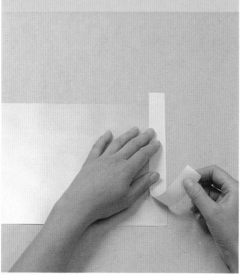

1

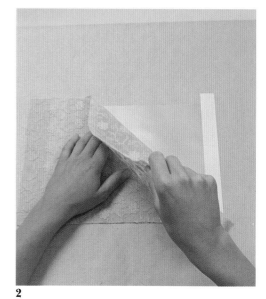

2

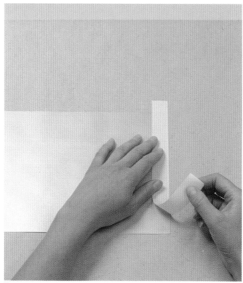

3

4

5 To create the lacy edges, use scrap paper to mask the area already sprayed, leaving uncovered one of the borders that was taped in step 1. Spray the back of the length of edging lace with low-tack adhesive, and position it at least 5mm (¼in) in from the exposed edge of the paper, allowing it to overlap onto the mask. Adjust this positioning if necessary, as you are trying to make the join between the two types of lace look as effortless as possible. Roll over the lace with a brayer, then spray the area with pale cream paint.

6 Peel the lace off before the paint is dry. Repeat on the opposite edge of the paper. Remove the lace and mask and leave the paper to dry completely.

7 Use the leather punch to make small round holes where appropriate in the lace pattern. Lay the edge of the sprayed paper on a kitchen sponge. Use the different-sized needles to pierce the paper where the lace pattern is most detailed. This will start to create the lace effect, which can be as detailed as you wish, or have time for.

8 Finally place the edge on a cutting mat and enhance the effect further by cutting out small areas with a craft knife.

9 To create the intricately shaped edge of the lace it is necessary to perforate it. Pierce holes very close together, following the edge of the lace pattern.

10 Very carefully, tear away the excess paper along the pierced line to reveal the delicate edge. Repeat along the opposite edge, then fold the paper accurately in half, lace edge to lace edge, decorated-side out.

5

6

7

8

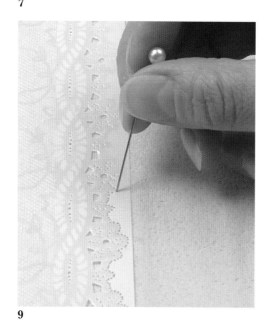

9

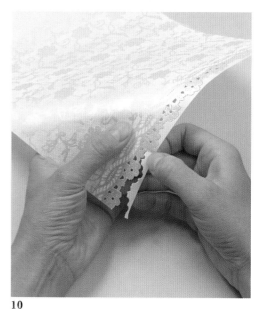

10

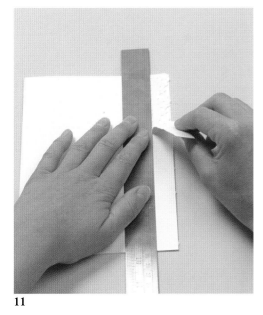

11

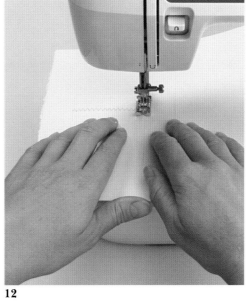

12

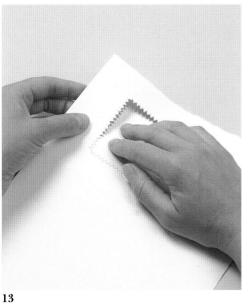

13

14

15

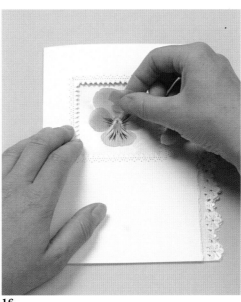

16

11 Place the lace internal sheet inside the folded card. Decide how much of the edge of the card to tear away to expose the edge of the lace design. Place a steel rule at this point, keeping it parallel to the edge, and tear away the excess card. Repeat on the back edge. Remove the internal sheet while you complete the card.

12 Using a pencil, lightly mark a 70 x 70mm (2¾ x 2¾in) square aperture centrally on the front of the card. Use a sewing machine with no thread in it to perforate around the aperture with a decorative stitch. Be careful to keep the pattern as fluent as possible at the corners. Practise first on some scrap paper. Gently rub out the pencil marks with a soft eraser.

13 Very carefully, push out the square of paper along the perforated lines to create a decorative aperture.

14 Frame the aperture with more lines of decorative perforations, using different stitches on the sewing machine.

15 Stick a length of narrow double-sided tape to the inside front of the card, against the fold. Remove the protective paper and stick the internal sheet in position.

16 To complete the card, apply a very light coat of spray adhesive on the back of the pansy and stick the flower to the front of the card, within the aperture.

Easter greetings

This woven Easter egg card is sweet enough to stand in for any chocolate egg, and has the advantage of being calorie-free!

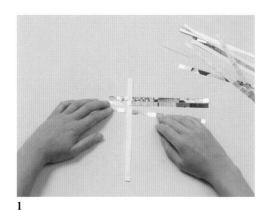

1

1 This is a perfect opportunity to recycle some of your favourite images from glossy magazines. Collect together a range of pretty papers of similar weights. Cut them up into 10mm- (½in-) wide strips on a guillotine if you have one, or using a craft knife and steel rule on a cutting mat. To start the weave off, place two strips of paper at right angles to each other. Position the next two strips, passing underneath a strip where you previously overlapped it and vice versa.

2 Continue to weave the strips together, passing alternate strips over and under, across and down to complete a piece of woven paper at least 150mm (6in) square.

3 Transfer the egg template onto the front of the card, positioning it at a jaunty angle. Open the card out flat on a cutting mat and carefully cut around the shape with the craft knife. Try to make the outline as smooth as possible. Rub out any pencil marks with a soft eraser.

2

3

4

4 Lay the card over the woven paper and, using the egg shape as a viewfinder, move it around until you find the most attractive area of weave. To give a sense of roundness to the egg, the woven strips are best positioned at a 45-degree angle to the upright egg. Mark the approximate position with a pencil around the outside edge of the card. Do not mark the card, or the woven paper within the aperture.

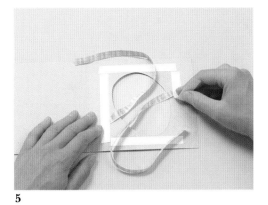

5

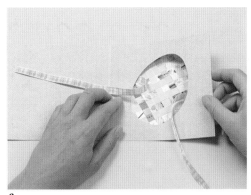

6

Getting it right
If you cut the magazine images up lengthways you will be able to make a woven piece large enough to make two or three cards.

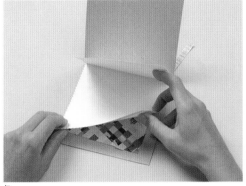

7

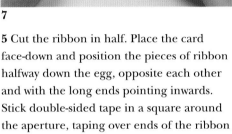

8

5 Cut the ribbon in half. Place the card face-down and position the pieces of ribbon halfway down the egg, opposite each other and with the long ends pointing inwards. Stick double-sided tape in a square around the aperture, taping over ends of the ribbon to hold them in place.

6 Pull the two free ends of ribbon through the egg to the right side. Peel the protective paper off the tape and position the card over the weave as marked in step 4. Press the card down so that the tape makes contact with the woven paper. Turn the card over and carefully trim the excess woven paper away from around the edges of the egg.

7 Trim the edges of the internal sheet with decorative scissors. To conceal the back of the woven paper and neaten the inside of the card, stick double-sided tape around the four edges of the sheet, on the side that will be against the inside front of the card. Peel the backing paper off the tape and stick the sheet in place inside the card.

8 On the front of the card, tie the ribbon in a bow and trim the ends into V-shapes.

21st birthday

This simple yet contemporary embossed card combines relief techniques to good effect. The numbers and motifs could be easily altered to suit other occasions.

1 Enlarge the templates so that the numbers measure 33mm (1⅛in) high and the star 25mm (1in) high. Transfer them onto the plain side of the medium-weight card and, using the craft knife and steel rule, cut them out on the cutting mat to make number and star stencils. Use the soft eraser to remove the remaining pencil marks. Cut a piece of blotting paper large enough to accommodate the numbers and a separate one to accommodate the star. Dampen the blotting paper and place it in the flower press with the stencils on top. Screw up the press and leave the blotting paper to dry.

2 Remove the embossed images from the press.

3 Cut the three embossed images into 40 x 40mm (1½ x 1½in) squares. Cut a fourth square the same size and punch out a star shape in the centre. Cut squares of the thick card, slightly smaller than the embossed squares.

4 To relief mount the punched motif, cut a small square out of the centre of one of the squares of thick card. Stick double-sided tape around the edges on both sides. Remove the protective paper on one side and stick the thick card to the back of the punched square, ensuring that it is not visible through the star. Mount the embossed squares onto the remaining squares of thick card and peel the protective paper off the tape.

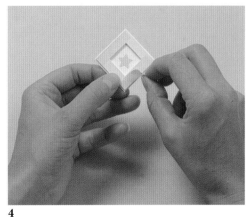

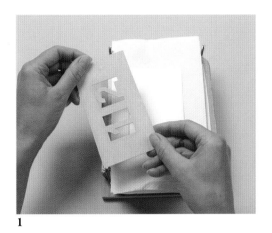

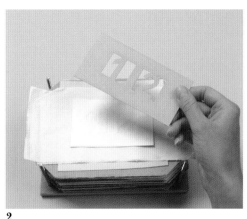

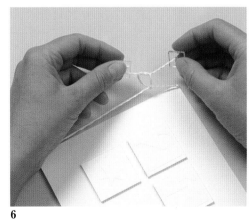

5 Mount the embossed and punched squares in a square on the card (see main picture).

6 Make a cord from the embroidery thread. Thread the buttons onto the ends of the cord, tie knots to secure them and trim off any excess. Knot the cord around the fold in the card.

Love token

The charm of this Valentine's card is that the copper heart can be taken off and hung up by its ribbon as a permanent reminder of your affections. The embossing technique used to decorate the copper is a variation of the piercing technique.

YOU WILL NEED

Heart template, page 156

Spray adhesive

Copper foil

Dried-up ballpoint pen

Scissors

Hole punch

Brown antiquing wax

Paper tissue

Letter templates, page 158

200 x 150mm (8 x 6in) soft-white single-fold card

Pencil

Tracing paper

Hand-sewing needle

Pin vice

Soft eraser

Strip of fabric

Craft knife

Steel ruler

TECHNIQUES

29 Spray adhesive, page 35

77 Piercing metal foil, page 78

4 Single-fold cards, page 17

40 Transferring a template, page 43

76 Piercing paper, page 76

68 Fraying fabric, page 70

1

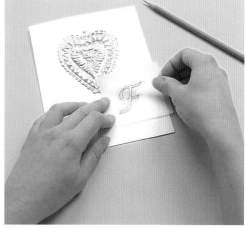

2

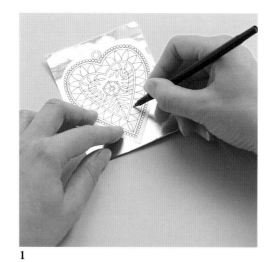

3

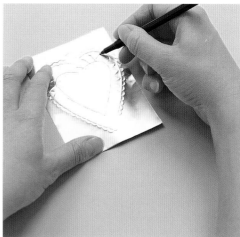

4

1 Enlarge the template so that the heart measures 100mm (4in) long. Cut it out and, using spray adhesive, stick the template to the copper foil. Lightly draw over the lines with a dried-up ballpoint pen.

2 Remove the template and firmly draw over the main heart lines and the scallops around the outside edge. Turn the copper foil over and draw over the rest of the lines from the other side to give a more defined effect.

3 Cut the heart out with scissors, and then punch a hole in the top to hang it from. Rub a little antiquing wax onto both sides of the heart. Rub the wax on with your finger, then buff it up with a paper tissue.

4 Enlarge the letter templates so that they measure 35mm (1½in) high. Place the heart on the front of the card and position the initials below it, one on either side. Transfer the initials onto the card.

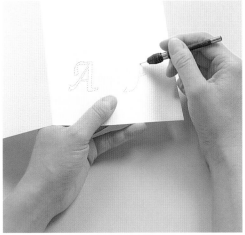

5

6

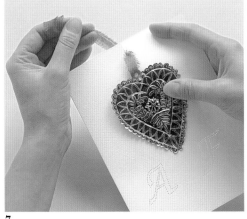

7

5 Pierce the initials with the needle, clamping it in a pin vice if you prefer. Follow the traced lines and space the holes evenly. Rub out the pencil lines with a soft eraser.

6 Fray the edges of a piece of fabric to make a strip approximately 10mm (½in) wide. Loop the fabric in half and thread the loop through the hole in the top of the heart. Take the ends of the fabric through the loop and pull it tight.

7 Cut a small slot in the top centre of the card and carefully slip the fabric into it, adjusting it until the heart hangs above and between the pierced initials.

Getting it right
If you are worried that the copper heart may be damaged in the post, give your love token personally.

Dinner party invitation

Set the scene for a delicious dinner with some elegant invitations that are quick to produce. You could use a computer to print out the date and details on cream paper and attach them inside the card as an internal sheet.

YOU WILL NEED

Vanilla light-weight card

Cutting mat

Craft knife

Steel rule

Thinners

Cotton bud

Black-and-white photocopied cutlery image

Teaspoon

100 x 150mm (4 x 6in) claret single-fold card

Leather punch

Eyelet and eyelet tool

Hammer

TECHNIQUES

13 Tearing against a rule, page 25

43 Photocopies and thinners, page 46

4 Single-fold cards, page 17

31 Eyelets, page 36

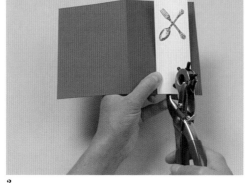

1

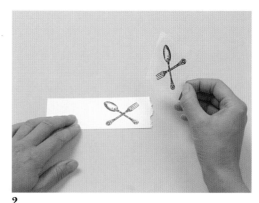

2

3

4

1 Place the vanilla card on a cutting mat and use a craft knife and steel rule to trim it into a 150 x 50mm (6 x 2in) strip. Position the steel rule 10mm (½in) from the right-hand short edge and tear the card against it.

2 Apply thinners to the back of the photocopy and transfer the image onto the vanilla card, positioning it towards the torn edge.

3 The card is used tent-style, with the crease running along the top edge. Position the vanilla strip 15mm (¾in) up from the bottom, matching the short straight edge against the left-hand edge of the card. Use a leather punch to make a hole through the two layers, where the eyelet will hold them together.

4 Pass the eyelet through the hole, from front to back, and hammer it open.

△ *Adapt the idea to make individual place-cards for your guests. If you have the facility to reverse type on your computer, you can transfer their names using the same technique. If not, use your best handwriting.*

Happy Halloween

Make an event of Halloween and treat children to a Jack o'Lantern card. For an extra surprise that appears at night, the images have been stamped and detailed with glow-in-the-dark paints! Once the pumpkin stamp has been prepared, the card is quick to make, which means that you can easily produce a number of them.

YOU WILL NEED

150 x 150mm (6 x 6in) black single-fold card

Pinking shears

Yellow ready-mixed fluorescent paint

Small container

Glow-in-the-dark paint

Paintbrush

Moon stamp

Scrap of black card to make stars

Jack o'Lantern template, page 157

Tracing paper

Pencil

Kitchen sponge

Scissors

Hardboard

All-purpose adhesive

Orange ready-mixed acrylic paint

Star punch

Small stick-on wobbly eye

Yellow glow-in-the-dark dimensional paint

Jack o'Lantern sequins

Black sewing thread

Large-eyed needle

TECHNIQUES

4 Single-fold cards, page 17

12 Using decorative scissors, page 25

51 Simple stamping, page 53

54 Making a stamp from sponge, page 55

75 Punching shapes, page 76

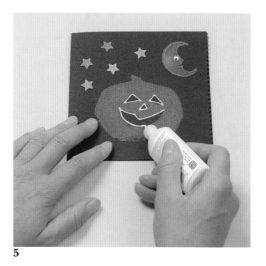

1

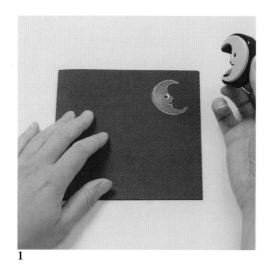

2

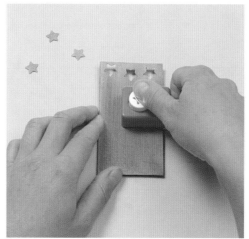

3

4

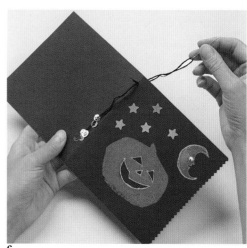

5

6

1 Trim the front edge of the card with pinking shears. Decant some yellow fluorescent paint into a small container and mix in some glow-in-the-dark paint. Brush this on to the moon stamp and stamp the image onto the top right-hand corner of the card. Paint the scrap of black card at the same time.

2 Using the template, make a Jack o'Lantern sponge stamp. Decant some orange acrylic paint into a small container and mix in some glow-in-the-dark paint. Brush it onto the sponge pumpkin stamp, then print the image onto the centre of the card. Leave it to dry.

3 Using the star punch, cut a number of stars from the painted scrap of card.

4 Use all-purpose adhesive to stick some stars to the card. Stick the wobbly eye onto the moon.

5 Outline the features of the Jack o'Lantern and the long back curve of the moon with yellow glow-in-the-dark dimensional paint. Leave to dry.

6 Tie several sequins onto lengths of thread. Bring the threads together and thread them all through the needle. Push the needle through the fold in the card, near the top. Tie the threads in a knot inside the card to secure the tassel.

△ *Use the same idea to make the trick-or-treat bag shown behind the card. Save a few clean paper carrier bags and spray them with black paint before decorating them. The glow-in-the-dark paint will really add to the effect as the children make their calls.*

Snow scene

Decorated with embossed sparkly snowflakes against an inky-blue sky, this is a quick and easy seasonal card that needs few materials. When folded, the card fits a standard-size envelope.

You will need

210 x 300mm (8¼ x 12in) piece of watercolour paper

Broad paintbrush

Water

Prussian blue artist's acrylic ink

Ruler

Bone folder

Snowflake rubber stamps

Clear embossing pad

White and silver sparkling embossing powder

Domestic iron

Fabric adhesive

220mm (8¾in) of white pom-pom braid

Techniques

34 Colourwashing with ink, page 38

5 Three-panel cards, page 18

91 Embossing with a stamp, page 90

24 Fabric adhesive, page 32

1 Using the broad paintbrush, apply water in a bold, undulating line across the paper, approximately a third of the way up. This line will form the skyline, with the unpainted area below suggesting a snowy landscape. Brush water roughly across the upper two-thirds of the paper. For the best results, do not work right to the edges and do not over-wet the paper.

2 Brush on the ink, allowing the colour to flood the wet area of the paper. Add more colour as required. The ink will gather in some areas, which will dry to a darker shade than other areas. The effect is random and will be different every time. Leave the paper to dry completely and, if necessary, place it under a few heavy books for a while to flatten it. Score and fold the paper to make a three-panel, concertina card.

3 Consider the best positions for the embossed snowflakes and stamp the motifs onto the card using the rubber stamps and the embossing pad. Allow some of the motifs to cross onto the white area; the sparkling powder will ensure they show up.

4 Sprinkle on the embossing powder and tip off the excess. Hold the card in front of the soleplate of a hot iron and let the powder melt and fuse together to complete the embossing process.

1

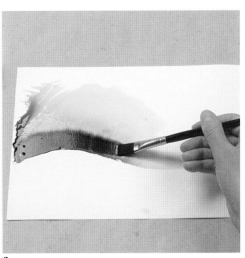

2

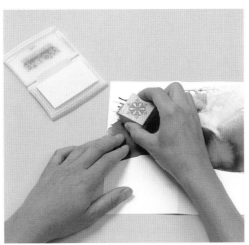

3

4

5 Apply fabric adhesive to the flat part of the pom-pom braid. Stick it to the back of the left-hand panel. Leave to dry and then trim the ends level with the top and bottom of the card.

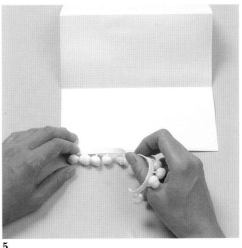

5

25th wedding anniversary

Celebrate a silver wedding with a flourish using metallic ink and accent beads. If you are unable to buy a card blank with a deckle edge, make your own by tearing the edges of a plain card.

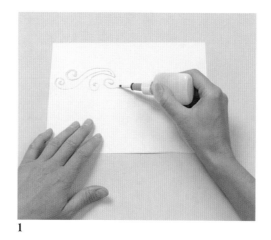

1

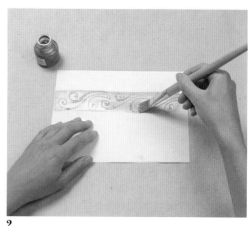

2

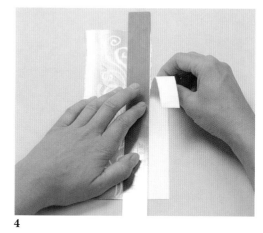

3

4

1 Use the applicator bottle to apply masking fluid across the watercolour paper in a series of freehand swirls, keeping them in a band approximately 40mm (1½in) deep. Leave the masking fluid to dry completely.

2 Brush silver ink over the paper in a strip approximately 65mm (2½in) deep, ensuring that you cover all of the masking fluid. Brush the ink on more thinly at the top and bottom edges to gradually fade the colour out. Leave to dry completely, then use your fingers to gently rub off and peel away the masking fluid.

3 Enlarge the number templates so that they measure 50mm (2in) high. Transfer them onto the double-sided film and cut them out with scissors. Peel off the backing paper and

stick them onto the decorated paper, positioning them to best effect on the pattern.

4 Make a panel 80mm (3in) deep by tearing the top and bottom edges of the decorated paper against a steel rule. The panel should stretch from edge to edge across the front of the card, so tear the right-hand edge to match the deckle edge of the card blank and cut the left-hand edge straight at the correct width. When tearing and cutting the panel, ensure that you keep the pattern and the numbers sensitively positioned within it.

5 Cut a piece of thick card slightly smaller than the decorated panel and stick double-sided tape around all edges on both sides. Peel the protective paper off the tape on one

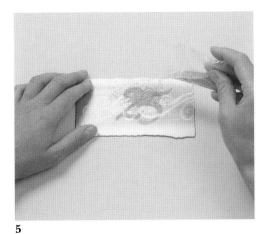

5

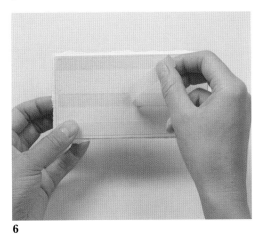

6

7

side and stick the thick card to the back of the panel. Peel the protective paper off the double-sided film numbers and sprinkle on accent beads, ensuring that they completely cover the film. Tip off the excess beads.

6 Remove the protective paper from the double-sided tape on the back of the thick card.

7 Position the panel carefully over the card, then press it down.

Butterfly card

Paper-cutting and iridescent embossing make the most of light and shadow and turn this simple motif into a striking card with an oriental flavour.

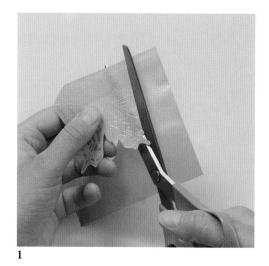

1

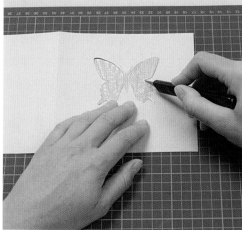

2

3

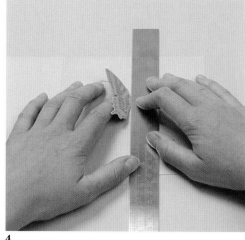

4

1 To create the butterfly, use the embossing pad and stamp the image onto the blue iridescent paper. Sprinkle pearl-blue embossing powder onto the wet butterfly image and hold it in front of the hot iron. Carefully cut out the embossed butterfly with sharp scissors.

2 Spray adhesive onto the back of the butterfly and stick it to the front of the card, positioning it as you wish. Cover the surface with plain scrap paper for protection and roll over the butterfly with the brayer to ensure that it is firmly stuck down.

3 Open the card out flat and place it on a cutting mat. Carefully cut round the edge of each wing with a craft knife. Do not cut out the body or antennae.

4 To create the relief effect, place a steel rule along the body of the butterfly, across the points where the wing is cut out. Press down firmly, while gently bending the wing up from the surface of the card to create a slight crease. Repeat with the other wing.

5 Trim and fold the gold pearlized paper to make an internal sheet. Stick it in place inside the card.

6 Make a cord from the embroidery thread. Thread beads onto the ends of the cord and tie knots to hold them in place. Apply a dab of all-purpose adhesive to the ends, then push them back up inside the beads.

5

6

Child's birthday

Use a range of simple techniques to make a personalized card that is sure to delight a special little girl. The idea can easily be adapted to suit a boy, or an older child, by changing the colour scheme and using an alternative braid.

You will need

White household candle

Large sheet of watercolour paper

Broad paintbrush

Process-magenta artist's acrylic ink

Cutting mat

Steel rule

Pencil

Craft knife

Bone folder

Initial button

Domestic iron

Fusible webbing

70mm (2¾in) square of yellow felt

Scissors

110mm (4½in) square of denim fabric

Pink yarn

Large-eyed needle

Fabric adhesive

Flower braid

Techniques

38 Wax resist, page 41

4 Single-fold cards, page 17

33 Fusible webbing, page 37

66 Hand appliqué, page 68

68 Fraying fabric, page 70

24 Fabric adhesive, page 32

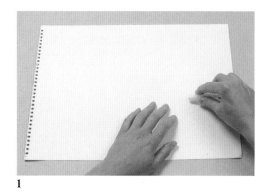

1

1 Using the candle, draw stripes across the surface of the watercolour paper.

2 Using the paintbrush, brush ink over the entire surface of the paper, either straight from the bottle, or diluting it first with a little water. Leave it to dry completely. Use this decorated paper to make a single-fold card that measures 200 x 150mm (8 x 6in) when it is folded.

3 Enlarge the initial button on a photocopier until it measures 60mm (2½in) high and cut it out. Iron the fusible webbing onto the felt. Lay the initial back to front on the webbing's paper backing and draw around it. Cut out the initial with scissors.

4 Peel off the backing paper and iron the initial onto the centre of the square of denim. Using pink yarn, appliqué the initial to the denim with random straight stitches. Fray the edges of the square approximately 10mm (½in) on each side.

5 Apply fabric adhesive to the back of the denim and stick it centrally onto the front of the card. Use fabric adhesive to stick a strip of braid along each side of the denim, immediately next to the frayed edges. Remove a few of the felt flowers from the braid and stick them to the initial for extra detail.

2

3

4

5

◁ Use another piece of the decorated paper
to make a matching gift tag, which the child
can keep and use as a bookmark. Cut a strip
of the decorated paper and embellish it with
a strip of frayed denim and some braid.
Make a cord in a co-ordinating yarn, punch
a hole in the centre of a short end of the
paper, loop the cord through the hole and
thread initial buttons onto the ends. A book
would then be the perfect gift!

Scented card

Scent adds a lovely dimension to this contemporary card.
It also offers a good way to stay in the memory of somebody
special, since they will undoubtedly keep the card on
display to perfume a room for a long time to come.

<small>You will need</small>

250mm (10in) of 70mm- (2¾in-)
wide ivory organza ribbon

Pins

Ivory thread

Beading needle

Lavender-coloured seed beads

Dried lavender particles

Sheet of scrap paper

200 x 150mm (8 x 6in) soft-white,
deckle-edged, single-fold card

Cutting mat

Steel rule

Craft knife

Pencil

Double-sided film

Scissors

Masking tape

Tweezers

Grey paper for internal sheet

Double-sided tape

<small>Techniques</small>

17 Beading edges, page 28

82 Attaching seeds and particles,
page 83

8 Internal sheets, page 21

Getting it right
This purchased card had a deckle-edge
and a matching tissue-lined envelope. If
you cannot buy a deckle-edged card,
tear an edge on a plain card.

1

2

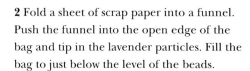

3

1 Fold the ribbon in half lengthways, and
measure 80mm (3in) up the sides from the
fold. Mark the measurements with pins.
Joining the two edges together as you stitch,
work beaded blanket stitch down one side,
from the pin to the fold. Continue stitching
and beading across the fold and back up the
other side, joining the edges as before, to the
pin. Make a few tiny whip stitches to secure
the thread and trim off the excess.

2 Fold a sheet of scrap paper into a funnel.
Push the funnel into the open edge of the
bag and tip in the lavender particles. Fill the
bag to just below the level of the beads.

3 Using tiny running stitches, hand-stitch the
top of the bag closed where the beads end.
Secure and trim the thread, as before.

4 Cut a horizontal slit in the front of the
card, 70mm (2¾in) long, positioned
centrally, and 55mm (2¼in) down from the
top edge of the card.

4

5 Stick a 70mm- (2¾in-) long, 3mm- (⅛in-) wide strip of double-sided film to the card, immediately above the slit.

6 Carefully push the raw ends of the lavender bag through the slit from the front. Turn the card over and level the bag. Trim off the excess ribbon and secure the top of the bag to the back of the card with masking tape.

7 Remove the protective paper from the double-sided film and use tweezers to position lavender particles in a neat row across the tape.

8 To neaten the inside of the card, make a torn-edge internal sheet, slightly smaller than the card. Stick double-sided tape around the edges of the side that will lie against the back of the card front. Remove the protective paper from the tape and stick the sheet in place.

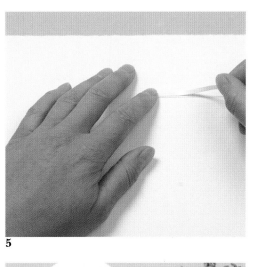

5

6

7

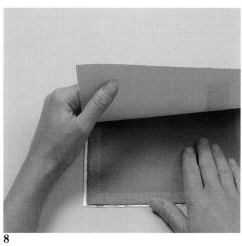

8

Elephant card

Colourful and exotic, this embellished elephant card reflects an Indian theme. It offers a wonderful opportunity of using up scraps of interesting papers and even bits of broken jewellery.

YOU WILL NEED

200 x 300mm (8 x 12in) piece of purple card

Pink mulberry paper

Spray adhesive

Brayer

Steel rule

Cutting mat

Craft knife

Stamp

Metallic gold ink pad

Bone folder

Soft eraser

Sewing machine

Gold machine-embroidery thread

Pink thin card

Assorted thin papers for collaged panel, including some gilded paper

L-crops

Pencil

Black-and-white photocopied elephant motif, page 157

Thinners

Cotton bud

Embroidery thread

Hand-sewing needle

Assorted coloured glass beads

Eyelet hole punch

Indian friendship bracelet or other soft bracelet

Gold and copper dimensional paint

TECHNIQUES

29 Spray adhesive, page 35

51 Simple stamping, page 53

4 Single-fold cards, page 17

18 Machine-stitching edges, page 29

84 Creating a background, page 84

43 Photocopies and thinners, page 46

16 Hand-stitching edges, page 27

1 Do not score or fold the card: this is best done later, as the pattern wraps around to the rear of the card. Tear random-sized paisley shapes out of the pink mulberry paper. Position them on the front of the card to form an even and balanced pattern that laps onto what will be the rear of the card. Do not worry about any bits that hang over the edge, these will be trimmed away after gluing; just concentrate on making the pattern look right. Use spray adhesive to attach the individual motifs, and roll across the surface with the brayer. Trim off the over-hanging edges.

2 Embellish the paisley shapes using the stamp and gold metallic ink pad. Leave to dry completely, then score and fold the card to make a 200 x 150mm (8 x 6in) single-fold card.

3 Use the sewing machine to decorate the edges of the card with a fancy stitch and metallic gold machine-embroidery thread.

4 Prepare a collaged panel by arranging several different papers on the pink card and then sticking them down with spray adhesive. Roll over them with the brayer to ensure that they are stuck down firmly. Use L-crops to select the best area and, using a craft knife and steel rule on a cutting mat, trim the collage to a panel measuring 120 x 85mm (4¾ x 3¼in).

5 Dab thinners onto the back of the photocopied elephant. Transfer the image onto the collaged panel, towards the bottom.

6 Decorate the edge of the collaged panel using whip-stitch. Measure, mark and pierce holes in the correct positions and add assorted coloured glass beads as you stitch. Stitch carefully around the corners, making sure that the front of the panel always looks neat.

7 Place the panel centrally on the front of the card, 30mm (1¼in) down from the top edge. Make two holes through the layers where the panel and card will be tied together. Use the tool from an eyelet kit to do this, as a leather punch won't reach. Space the holes far enough apart so the Indian friendship bracelet will sit in between the holes. Thread the ends of the cord through the holes and tie them together inside the card.

8 Pick out some of the detail on the elephant with dimensional paint. Leave to dry completely.

3

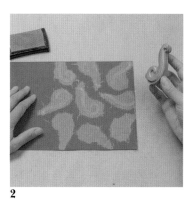
2

1

4

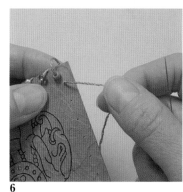
5

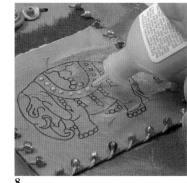
6

Christmas tree card

If every year you mean to make your own seasonal greetings cards, but never quite manage to find the time, then this is the project for you. You will spend longer writing and sealing them into envelopes than you did making the cards!

YOU WILL NEED

Cutting mat

Serrated knife

High density stencil sponge

White emulsion paint

Flat dish

210 x 100mm (8¼ x 4in) silver metallic single-fold card

Glue pen

Small coloured cup sequins

All-purpose adhesive

Gold star sequin

TECHNIQUES

51 Simple stamping, page 53

4 Single-fold cards, page 17

23 Glue pen, page 32

22 All-purpose adhesive, page 31

Getting it right

For speed, buy ready-made cards to decorate. Once you have cut the sponges and gathered the materials together, it's easiest to produce a run of cards in stages. Lay a number out on a work surface and print all the triangles, then all the pots and trunks. Leave them to dry, then stick on all the sequins and finally all the stars. What could be easier or quicker? Use the same technique to make gift wrap and tags for a fully co-ordinated look.

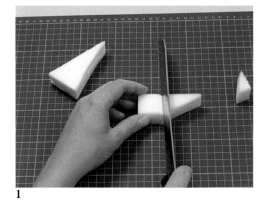

1

2

3

4

5

1 Working on a cutting mat, use a serrated knife to cut the sponge into an elongated triangle to make a simple Christmas tree shape 90mm (3½in) tall and 50mm (2in) across at the base. From the off cuts, cut a 25 x 25mm (1 x 1in) square, which will make the base and the trunk of the tree.

2 Decant some white paint into a flat dish and spread it out thinly. Dip the face of the triangular sponge into the paint, ensuring that the surface is evenly covered.

3 Press the triangle onto the front of the card, positioning it centrally and with the point approximately 40mm (1½in) down from the top. Gently lift the sponge off the card, being careful not to smudge the print.

4 Coat the face of the square sponge by dipping it into the white paint. Make the pot

by stamping a square centrally, about 10mm (½in) below the tree. The trunk is made with the same square sponge held at an angle to make a narrow line, joining the tree to the pot. Leave to dry completely.

5 Use a glue pen to stick on a few sequin baubles and a dab of all-purpose adhesive to attach the star to the top of the tree.

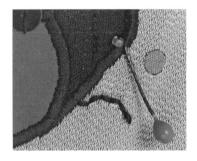

Ladybird card

Machine appliqué and hand-stitched details are needed to bring this lucky seven-spotted ladybird to life. This one is emerging from the camouflage of red and black spotted silk, but would look equally good crawling across a grass-green background.

YOU WILL NEED

Ladybird templates, page 157

Black woven iron-on interfacing

Pins

Scissors

Domestic iron

Fusible webbing

Red cotton velveteen

Iron-on interfacing

180 x 180mm (7 x 7in) square of spotted silk

Embroidery hoop

Sewing machine

Black machine thread

Double-ended artificial flower stamen

Black embroidery thread

Hand-sewing needle

Black sequins

Two clear glass seed beads

Double-sided tape

150 x 150mm (6 x 6in) green single-fold card

TECHNIQUES

33 Fusible webbing, page 37

67 Machine appliqué, page 69

68 Fraying fabric, page 70

26 Double-sided tape, page 33

4 Single-fold cards, page 17

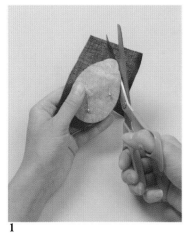

1

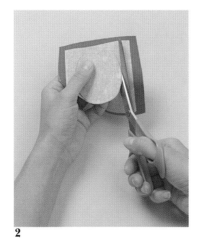

2

3

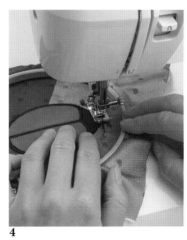

4

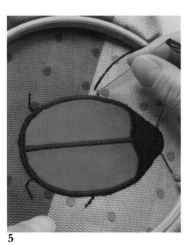

5

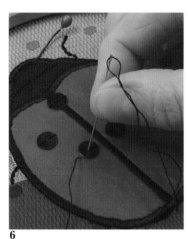

6

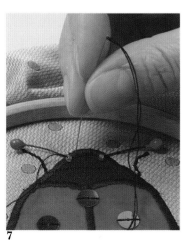

7

8

1 The ladybird's body is made from two layers of fabric, the large black head and thorax and the smaller red wings. Enlarge the templates so that the head measures 90mm (3½in) long and the wings 70mm (2¾in) long down the centre line. Cut the templates out and pin the larger one to the black interfacing. Cut out the shape with scissors.

2 Iron fusible webbing to the back of the red velveteen and pin the smaller pattern onto the paper backing. Draw around it then cut it out. Iron a 110mm (4½in) square of interfacing to the wrong side of the silk fabric, covering the area where the ladybird will be. Position the black body on the right side of the silk and iron it on. Peel the protective backing paper off the velveteen and iron it on top of the black body. Fasten the silk into an embroidery hoop.

3 The outline is stitched in two stages. With the machine set on a wide satin stitch and using black thread, first stitch around the edge of the head, starting and finishing at the red fabric. Then stitch all around the red wings. Bisect the wings with a line of stitching up the centre.

4 Hold the flower stamen centrally on the top of the satin stitch at the top of the head and attach it, using the same stitch, to make the antennae. Stitch over approximately 15mm (¾in) of the stamen,

working exactly over the previous line of satin stitch. Set the machine to straight stitch and stitch a line approximately half way down the black area to make a division between the head and thorax.

5 Use backstitch and black embroidery thread to add six short legs. Make them slightly crooked, so that the ladybird looks as though it is crawling along.

6 Stitch the seven sequins in place, using the main photograph as a guide to the positions. Bring the needle up through the middle of a sequin and down at the side of it. Repeat this, bringing the needle down through the fabric on the other side of the sequin.

7 Sew on bead eyes, one on either side of the antennae.

8 Remove the embroidery hoop and press the edges of the silk flat. Cut it into a 130 x 130mm (5 x 5in) square and fray the edges 5mm (¼in) on each side. Stick strips of double-sided tape to the silk, just inside the frayed edges. Peel off the protective paper and stick the square centrally on the front of the card.

Getting it right
Flower stamens are usually white with red ends, so blacken the white with a felt-tip pen. If you can't get black iron-on interfacing, iron fusible webbing onto the back of black cotton. This will work just as well.

Picture card

This tongue-in-cheek play on a formal portrait is a great way to present a cute photograph of a loved one to family or friends. Create an 'old master' of your own with a photograph of a pet or a favourite view.

Getting it right

If you are worried about the acetate moving as you stitch, hold it in place with small pieces of masking tape. Remove them carefully when you have finished stitching.

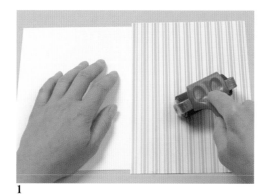

1

2

3

4

5

1 Cut the striped paper a bit bigger than the front of the card. Spray adhesive onto the back and position it on the front of the opened-out card, with the left-hand edge butted up to the fold. Roll a brayer across the surface to ensure that the paper is stuck down.

2 Place the card face-down on a cutting mat. Using a craft knife and steel rule, cut around three sides of the front of the card, trimming away the excess striped paper.

3 Enlarge the template so that the inside of the frame measures 100mm (4in) high. Photocopy the enlarged template onto the acetate. Cut around the outer edge of the frame, approximately 3mm (⅛in) from the edge of the image. Don't worry about cutting exactly around all the intricate detail, the cut edge will be almost invisible against the striped background.

4 Position the frame on the front of the card, ink-side down, and hold it firmly in place. Use a sewing machine threaded with invisible thread to stitch around the top, right-hand and bottom sides of the inner frame. The left-hand side, nearest the fold, remains open to insert the photograph.

5 Trim the photograph to fit comfortably inside the frame. Slide it into place through the open side.

Fish card

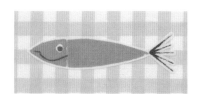

Fish for compliments with this fabric-based card that requires no sewing. You can use another printed fabric motif, such as flowers, if you prefer.

1

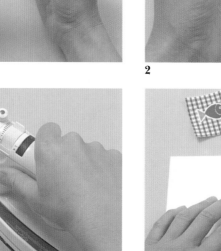

2

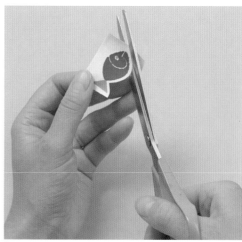

3

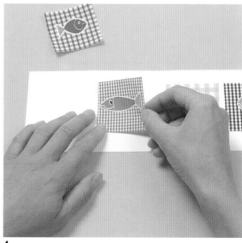

4

1 This card, despite its unusual shape, fits a standard-size envelope. It is 100mm (4in) high, the largest panel is 210mm (8½in) long, and the two shorter ones are each 70mm (2¾in) long. Mark these distances and then score and fold the panels to make a concertina-style card.

2 Iron fusible webbing onto the back of the printed fish and cut them out with sharp scissors. For a card of these dimensions, the motifs must fit within 60mm (2½in) squares.

3 Apply iron-on interfacing to the back of the gingham fabrics and cut out five 60 x 60mm

(2½ x 2½in) squares. Peel the backing paper off the fusible webbing and iron the motifs onto the gingham squares.

4 Using fabric adhesive, stick the gingham squares to the card. Stick one on each of the small panels and three across the long panel, positioning them evenly across the space.

5 Thread the fish buttons onto the transparent elastic.

6 Using a needle, pierce holes in the card, one 10mm (½in) from the top edge on the forward-facing crease, and one 10mm (½in)

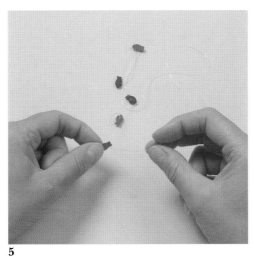

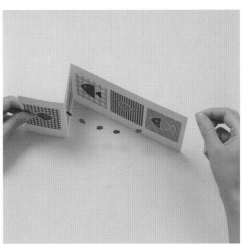

◁ To make the matching gift tag shown in front of the card, fold a strip of watercolour paper in half and apply a fish motif to it in the same way as the card. Punch a hole near the fold and loop a length of fishing line through it. Thread a fish button onto the line and attach the tag to the gift.

down and 10mm (½in) in from the top-right corner of the long panel. Thread the elastic through one of the holes and knot it on the back. Thread the other end through the remaining hole and fold the card closed. Pull the elastic through, so that the threaded buttons do not hang below the lower edge of the card while it is closed, and knot it at the back. The elastic stretches enough to allow the card to be opened out flat.

5

6

Wedding invitation

This invitation is simple and fast to make, offering a viable and much more personal alternative to a bought card. Use a computer to print the details on the internal sheet, or have them prepared at a copy-shop, and co-ordinate the accent colour with the wedding scheme.

YOU WILL NEED

200 x 150mm (8 x 6in) white, ribbed, single-fold card

Silver ink pad

Flower punch

Purchased lilac velvet flower motif

Fabric adhesive

Piece of 200 x 287mm (8 x 11¼in) light-weight lilac paper

Glue stick

500mm (20in) of 3mm- (⅛in-) wide silver ribbon

Scissors

TECHNIQUES

4 Single-fold cards, page 17

75 Punching shapes, page 76

24 Fabric adhesive, page 32

8 Internal sheets, page 21

21 Paper adhesive, page 31

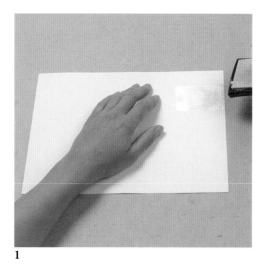

1

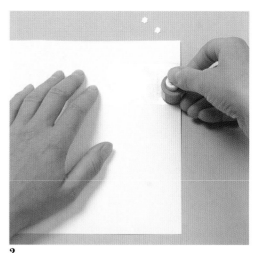

2

1 Lay the opened-out card flat on some scrap paper. This will protect the work surface and allow the silver panel to bleed off the right-hand edge. Press the ink pad onto the front of the card, approximately 30mm (1¼in) down from the top edge. Leave to dry.

2 Slide the edge of the card into the punch and punch out three flowers in a row, all within the silver panel.

3 Apply a little fabric adhesive to the back of the velvet flower and stick it to the card, positioning it towards the left of the silver panel, so that it balances the punched motifs.

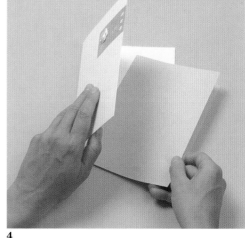

3

4 The internal sheet is slightly smaller than the card, but it covers the back of the cut-out motifs, allowing the colour to show through. Use a glue-stick to apply a thin line of adhesive next to the fold on the inside front of the card. Hold the card half-closed and slide the internal sheet into place. Close the card and the sheet will stick to the adhesive in the correct position.

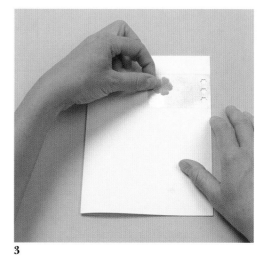

4

5 Finish the card by knotting a length of narrow silver ribbon around the fold, trimming the ends at an angle.

Getting it right

If you are making a number of cards, buy card blanks and spend an enjoyable and creative evening with your betrothed or best friend. Get a mini production line going: one of you stamps, while the other punches, and so on. The idea could easily be developed to include other wedding stationery, such as orders of service, place cards and thank-you notes.

5

Templates

On this page are templates for three standard shapes for flat envelopes (see *9 Envelopes from templates*, page 22), and two shapes for pillow envelopes (see *11 Pillow envelopes*, page 24).

Some techniques have used specific motifs, which are on page 155. You do not need to use the same motifs, but they are here if you want them. Several of the projects also use motifs and you will find these on pages 156–158.

To use any of the templates or motifs, first enlarge it on a photocopier to the required size. Follow *4o Transferring a template* (see page 43) to transfer the template onto a card.

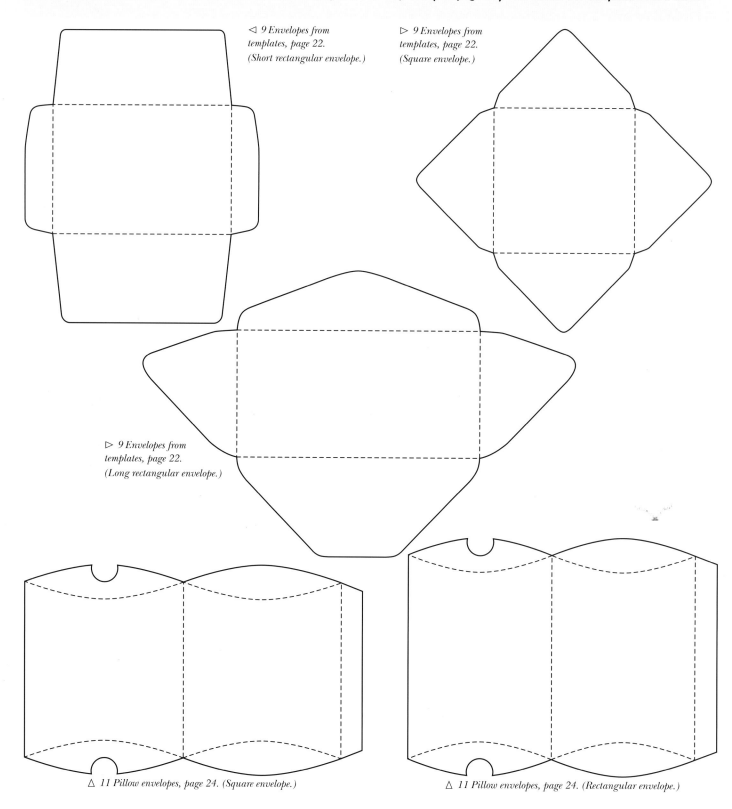

◁ *9 Envelopes from templates, page 22. (Short rectangular envelope.)*

▷ *9 Envelopes from templates, page 22. (Square envelope.)*

▷ *9 Envelopes from templates, page 22. (Long rectangular envelope.)*

△ *11 Pillow envelopes, page 24. (Square envelope.)*

△ *11 Pillow envelopes, page 24. (Rectangular envelope.)*

△ *Sticking and fixing, pages 31–37.*

40 Transferring a template, page 43

▽ *50 Masking and spraying, page 52.*

△ *45 Embellishing a stencil, page 48.*

△ *53 Making a stamp from string, page 54.*

△ *54 Making a stamp from sponge, page 55.*

△ *76 Piercing paper, page 76.*

△ *76 Piercing paper, page 76.*

△ *76 Piercing paper, page 76.*

△ *77 Piercing metal foil, page 78.*

△ *88 Embossing with a stencil, page 87.*

△ *93 Gilding with a size pen, page 92.*

△ *97 Paper-cutting, page 96.*

◁ ▽ *Pop-up valentine, page 110.*

▷ *Easter Greetings, page 122.*

△ *21st birthday, page 124.*

◁ *Love token, page 126.*

△ *Dinner party invitation, page 128.*

△ *Happy Halloween,*
page 130.

△ *Elephant card, page 142.*

△ ▽ *Ladybird card, page 146.*

△ *Picture card, page 148.*

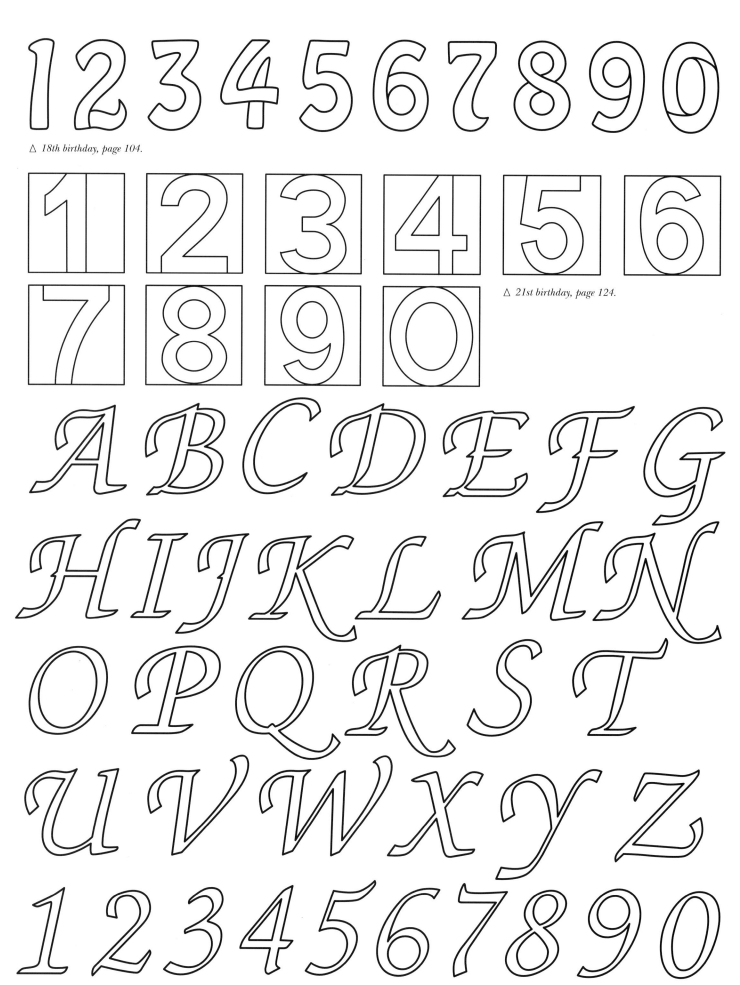

△ *18th birthday, page 104.*

△ *21st birthday, page 124.*

△ *Love token, page 126, and 25th wedding anniversary, page 134.*

Suppliers

UK

Alec Tiranti Limited
Suppliers of gilding materials and metal leaf.
Mail-order service.
70 High Street
Theale, Reading
Berkshire RG7 5AR
Tel: 0118 930 2775
Email: enquiries@tiranti.co.uk

Celestial
Retailers of designer buttons and trimmings.
162 Archway Road
London N6 5BB
Tel: 020 8341 2788

Craft Creations
Greetings cards blanks and accessories.
Mail-order service.
Ingersoll House
Delamare Road, Cheshunt
Hertfordshire EN8 9HD
Tel: 01922 781 900
Email: enquiries@craftcreations.com
Web: www.craftcreations.com

The Cutting Edge
The Cutting Edge offer a large range of ready-made
card blanks and supply paper and envelopes that are
recycled or sourced from 'greener' manufacturers.
They also supply a growing range of equipment and
materials including embossing powders, rubber
stamps, paper punches, craft knives, decorative-edge
scissors and re-moistenable adhesive.
Unit 17a, C.E.C.
Mill Lane, Coppull
Lancashire PR7 5BW
Tel: 01257 792025
Email: sales@eco-craft.co.uk
Web: www.eco-craft.co.uk

Hobbycraft
Art and craft superstores.
Tel: 0800 0272387 for your nearest branch

Lakeland Limited
Carry a small range of craft materials and
equipment, including real pressed-flower stickers.
Tel: 015394 88100 for your nearest branch or
a catalogue.

In addition the following wholesale suppliers
distribute quality materials, some of which
have been used in this book, to many art and
craft stores across the country. Do ask about
their products in your local craft store.

Robert Horne Paper
Art materials and a range of interesting papers.

R.K.Burt & Company Ltd
A wide range of specialist papers, quality card
blanks and stationery.

USA

Kate's Paperie
Retailers of all types of paper and card blanks.
561 Broadway
New York, NY 10012
Tel: 888 941 9169
Web: www.katespaperie.com

Pearl Paint Co Inc
Retailers of art and craft materials.
308 Canal Street
New York, NY 10013
Tel: 800 451 PEARL
Web: www.pearlpaint.com

Swallow Creek Papers
Retailers of fine papers.
PO Box 152
Spring Mills, PA 16875
Tel: 814 422 8651

Flax Art & Design
Papers and card making equipment.
1699 Market Street
San Francisco, CA 94103
Tel: 415 552 2355
Web: www.flaxart.com

Michaels
Art and craft materials of all kinds.
Tel: 800 642 4235
Web: www.michaels.com

Author's acknowledgements

I would like to sincerely thank the team involved in the production of this book for making it such a pleasurable and rewarding experience; I can't help but feel proud of the outcome!

Firstly, thanks to Kate Haxell, my editor, for extending the opportunity to turn a pipe dream into reality. You are a paragon, personally and professionally. To Kate Kirby at Collins & Brown, for trusting in the judgement of my editor! To the lovely Matt Dickens, whose skills as a photographer are evident, but whose constant patience and calming influence might be more difficult to discern! To Roger Daniels, the designer, who managed to make everything fit on the pages and still look beautiful. To Shirley, for being a great hand model.

My thanks also to Kevin McCarthy at The Cutting Edge for bending over backwards to accommodate my materials and equipment needs, and always with good grace and interest.

To the Robert Horne Group, particularly Peter Lewis and the Birmingham branch, for supplying exciting and interesting paper stock. Also to Clifford Burt of R.K.Burt & Company Ltd for providing special papers and glorious ready-made card blanks and envelopes.

On a personal note, enormous thanks and gratitude to my sister, Emma, for her clear vision, practical common sense and creative input, and for providing me with two gorgeous nieces! To my family, old and new – especially my Mum and Dad – and the many friends who have made this project possible by supporting and helping in countless ways including dog-sitting, baby-sitting, shopping, cleaning and generally encouraging me. Thank you so much. Finally, to Ady, for love, constancy and passionate belief.

Publisher's acknowledgements

Some of the motifs used in this book were taken from *The Crafter's Pattern Sourcebook* by Mary MacCarthy (Collins & Brown) and *The Glass Painter's Motif Library* by Alan D Gear and Barry L Freestone (Collins & Brown).

Index